American
Film Directors

FRANKLIN WATTS
NEW YORK | LONDON | 1976

Ronald Lloyd

American
Film
Directors

The World
As They See It

Photographs courtesy of the
Lester Glassner Collection.

Library of Congress Cataloging in Publication Data

————.
   American film directors.

   Includes index.
   SUMMARY: Examines the work of six major
American film directors and, more briefly, several
newer directors.
   1. Moving-picture producers and directors—
United States—Juvenile literature. [1. Motion
picture producers and directors] I. Title.
PN1998.A2F76   791.43'0233'0922   75-37949
ISBN 0-531-01110-0

Contents

American Film Directors

The Dream-makers

Movies are like the dreams we might have when we are awake. Like dreams they seem real while they happen, but afterward we realize that they are not entirely true. Movies make use of the basic raw material of our waking world but somehow transform it into a more exciting, more intense experience. Films resemble dreams in another way as well. They both have a unique language and structure. As there is a distorted "dream logic," there is a similar "film logic" that disrupts time and transcends space, and has the freedom to reorganize the elements of ordinary life according to rules unknown in the usual waking state.

The camera can shatter time as it cuts forward and flashes back, compresses a day into a breathless few minutes, or extends an agonizing second for what may seem like hours. It can break all barriers of space, span continents and galaxies, change geographies in the flash of an eye. Most of all, the motion picture, like the dream, gives us another reality into which to escape from the occasional boredom and frustration of the daily world.

The conditions necessary to watch a movie resemble the preparations for sleep. The lights go out, and you relax into a safe darkness that isolates you from everything else. All visual and aural distractions are excluded. You sit, anonymously among strangers, ready to lose yourself in the images about to fill the screen. Conscious anticipation slowly changes into unconscious involvement with illusions that have the power to upset or exhilarate you long after you leave the theater. It is the power of a manufactured reality that takes the world we know and magnifies and deepens it.

To a great extent movies, like dreams, fulfill our most secret desires and fears. In this way they serve the same function as the great myths of the past. Films like *Rosemary's Baby* and *The Exorcist* appeal to the same fascination and dread of the supernatural that we find in primitive religions. The stylized violence of *Bonnie and Clyde* and *The Wild Bunch* satisfies our deep need to play out in fantasy destructive instincts—the same need that was felt by audiences who listened to Homer's bloody tales of the Trojan War. Films of romance and sexual adventure are to us what the poems describing the amorous exploits of the young god Krishna have been to the Hindu people. In Elizabethan England people went to the theater to share vicariously in the lives of the rich and powerful; to be transported through words, as we are through images, to another place and time; to live, if only for a few hours, a dream of opulence and high drama. It is no different for us. We fall in love with Robert Redford, step coolly into the street like Bogart, hate Jack Palance, wonder what a night with Ali MacGraw would be like. The heroes and villains of the screen are people we might or might not want to meet or be, but they do satisfy our private longings in some mysterious way.

Myths are the collective dreams of a people, and they help that people to organize and interpret reality. This is another reason that we go to the movies. Our own lives are confused and chaotic, often beyond our control. Things happen at random, without apparent purpose or meaning. We are driven by impulses we don't understand, and we react in ways that seem to make no sense. Even our dreams, though we create them, may puzzle and frighten us. Watching a movie is a more satisfactory experience. It touches us, deals with the basic elements of our waking lives, but it does so in a coherent way.

From the opening credits we know that someone is in charge. Nothing will happen that is not meant to happen or that will go unexplained. Order will be imposed on what is usually chaos. Our emotions will be stirred, but to some end, according to some intelligible plan. We soon recognize that a certain character may undergo terrible trials but will not be killed. If he is, and no good reason is given, we feel that our sympathies have been abused. This is the weakness of *Chinatown*, in which Faye Dunaway is pointlessly killed. If two characters fall in love, we assume that, although thwarted, they will come together at the end. If they do not, we expect to understand why. We accept the break-up of Richard Benjamin and Ali MacGraw in *Goodbye Columbus* and must have Dustin Hoffman and Katherine Ross reconciled in *The Graduate*. We willingly participate in war, crime, espionage, romance, and adventure because we know that there is a benevolent "god" who will make sense of it all or make it come out as we wish it to be. If a film does portray life as it is, it will do so in order to give us greater insight into why life is that way. We will leave the theater refreshed and, one hopes, somewhat wiser.

If films are dreams created for us by others, who makes them? Often it is hard to tell. Movies are the only art form created by committee. Playwrights or composers or choreographers, although working in the performing arts, work alone. Others present their work, essentially intact. For directors this is not so. Not only must they rely on dozens of people to produce their work, they frequently have little control over what appears on the screen. There are thousands of cases where the film a director made and the one we see bear little resemblance to each other—the film has been cut to bits in the editing room, its scenes shortened and rearranged or new scenes inserted, and its characters and plot changed entirely. Occasionally a director is taken off a film and another one hired to complete it.

Even under the most ideal conditions, a director must work under tremendous handicaps. Most directors cannot make any film they want to. They are offered a choice of scripts that a producer—the person who provides the money—thinks will be commercial successes. Directors often cannot choose the actors they want but must make do with people assigned to them, because they either are popular or available or will work for the money budgeted. Even while filming, the director must be constantly aware of the current taste of the movie-going public and of the possibility of censorship, and of what distributors, exporters to foreign countries, and theater owners think will sell. No matter how fine a film may be, it will not be made if a large enough audience cannot be expected to come to see it.

Once on location the work of directing a film is almost impossibly frustrating. There are the various talents and temperaments of a small army of technicians and specialists to contend with, many of whom may not fully understand what the director is trying to do. Script writers, cameramen, lighting experts, set designers, costumers, hairdressers, cosmeticians, carpenters, grips, production assistants, the film editor (if the director is not cutting the movie himself), the composer who will score the movie, the actors and actresses, and often the producer are all on the scene. Anyone who has seen François Truffaut's *Day for Night* or Federico Fellini's *8½* can begin to understand the problems involved. And yet, when the film is finished, it bears the director's name. Whatever the outcome, the director is held responsible. It is a testimony to the skill and determination of certain directors that, against all odds, they have impressed their distinctive personal stamp on such a collective enterprise.

It is only recently that we have come to accept this *auteur* theory of film—that is, that the director is in fact the "author" of the film. In the past, movies were identified primarily by their star, a Cagney or Fairbanks or Garbo, or by their type, a comedy or musical or gangster film. Only a few directors like D. W. Griffith or Charles Chaplin or Ernst Lubitsch were recognized as having made them. But in the 1950s the young critics of the French film journal *Cahiers du Cinema* (many of them—François Truffaut, Jean-Luc Godard, Claude Chabrol, Eric Rohmer, and Alain Resnais—now film-makers themselves) began to consider the entire body of a particular director's work, and saw a consistency of style and technique, an overriding point of view that existed regardless of subject, actors, or the confused conditions under which the films were made.

Thus, the films of John Ford, when taken all together, are not simply Westerns, but are films, on Western themes, that contain a personal philosophy and a highly original approach to film-making. Whether Orson Welles is making a pathetically low-budget film of *Othello,* an expensive psychological mystery like *Citizen Kane,* or a commercial potboiler like *Touch of Evil,* there is a distinctive use of camera and light and a concern with certain human values that make all these seemingly different films unquestionably his. An Alfred Hitchcock movie is no longer considered simply a dependably terrifying thriller, but a film that will bear the recognizable mark of his psychological insight and technical genius.

By splicing together pieces of film that will be sped through a projector at twenty-four frames a second, these men, like all original artists, help us to know ourselves and our world in a new way. They supply us with daydreams, not only for entertainment and escape, but so that we may feel more deeply and see more clearly. They have given us their personal vision through illusory images that equal literature, music, and art in their power to move us. In order to appreciate and be changed by these images we must be willing to investigate how they were made as well as what they may mean.

John Ford

In the Ford tradition, a sense of duty forces three men to ride in search of a young girl kidnaped by renegade Indians. From left to right above, Harry Carey, Jr., Jeffrey Hunter, and John Wayne in The Searchers (1956). At right, the Ford hero senses his responsibility to protect the home and community he can never be a part of. (From The Searchers.)

The conflict in human characters is shown in Stagecoach *(1939).
From left to right above, a gambler (John Carradine), a whiskey
salesman (Donald Meek), and Doc Boone (Thomas Mitchell).
At right: a sense of mutual responsibility emerges when the
group is faced with an Indian attack. From left to right, George
Bancroft, John Carradine, Donald Meek, Louise Platt, Claire
Trevor, and John Wayne.*

☆ 21

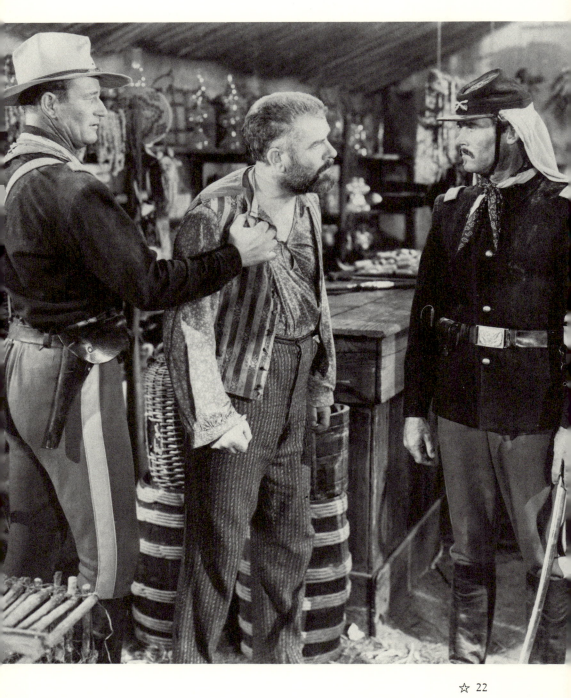

The Ford hero (Wayne) and his opposite (Henry Fonda) at left in Fort Apache *(1948). The man in the center is Grant Withers. Above:* The Informer *(1935) tells the story of an inarticulate man who cannot express his guilt. The film is a good example of Ford's use of symbolic image. Tom Sawyer (on the left) suspects that Victor McLaglen (on the right) is the real informer.*

☆ 23

The first image in *The Searchers* (1956) is the silhouette of a woman who is standing in the cool, dark doorway of a frontier cabin and looking out into the searing heat and sun of the desert. As she stoically waits, a man rides up, wearily dismounts, and walks slowly toward her. We are in John Ford country, and all the elements are there. Pictorially, it is a scene of stark contrasts, light in conflict with dark, interior pitted against exterior, the figures sharply etched in their solitude, the implacable outlines of a harsh environment looming behind them. The people are dramatic, larger than life, and what happens to them has the force and fatality of history recorded on the screen.

The woman, Martha Edwards, like most Ford women, stands powerfully against all that would threaten home and family. Sheltered inside, she represents peace, comfort, and the fragile stability of civilization. Like Ma Joad in *The Grapes of Wrath* (1940) and Mrs. Morgan in *How Green Was My Valley* (1941), she has the quiet, steady strength traditionally assigned to women of endurance, patience, and self-sacrifice. She is protected from sun and wind and cold by a flimsy house her men have built and from the destruction of her carefully ordered world by those same men. In her turn she sustains them, gives their struggle meaning, and usually outlives them to carry on what they have died to preserve.

The man, her brother-in-law Ethan Edwards, one of the many Ford roles played by John Wayne, is the typical Ford hero. He is a wanderer and outsider who serves a society he cannot himself live in. He respects the values of that society, the domestic virtues of home and community, but he is driven by a higher call to duty. He is independent, self-reliant, more physical than intellectual, expresses himself more through gestures than words, and is not afraid to use violence when it is required. He drinks hard, fights hard, lives hard, and remains always alone. Living outside the law of society, he embodies the spirit of that law by adhering to a strict personal code of moral behavior and an almost religious respect for ritual and honor. He is an ordinary human being raised to the stature of hero through his courageous acceptance of a situation that he cannot, as a self-respecting man, avoid. He usually dies. He is almost always defeated. But the proof of his heroism is his private victory in the face of defeat.

In *Fort Apache* (1948) Captain Kirby York, played by John Wayne, and Colonel Owen Thursday, played by Henry Fonda, are examples of the Ford hero and his opposite. York is a passionate, outgoing man, proud, flexible, sympathetic to his soldiers, gallant to women, living by a personal code of conduct that is a natural part of him. When he observes military discipline, it is because he understands its value, and his inherent respect for it allows him to depart from it when necessary. He fights from a sense of duty, not for personal gain, and is willing to sacrifice himself for others. He respects the enemy—the Indian—and the terrain he must fight on. He has the humility and humor of the typical Ford leader.

Thursday is a cold, arrogant officer who lives by the book. He applies the rules without understanding them. He is driven by ambition and too high an opinion of himself. His arrogance causes him to willfully disregard the accepted rules of society and to underestimate the dangers of his job. He considers himself superior to society, war, and nature. He has contempt for the fighting ability of the Indians, the difficulties of the terrain, his own men. In an attempt to become famous, he imposes his will on man and nature alike, and is doomed to lose. The exact quality of his failure is shown visually in his last battle. Refusing all advice, he charges his men up a closed box canyon into an ambush which annihilates his command.

Thursday is a fool, but not a villain, in Ford's moral universe. The villains are those people who threaten the basic foundations of society. The coward, because he cannot be relied on to protect it. And the dishonest, because the community depends on absolute trust between its members. Ford admires the frontier, because life there is based on personal honor, not rigid law, and because the citizens of the frontier community must subserve their individual interests to the good of the whole in order to survive. The self-seeking, the greedy, the money-hungry, the ambitious are bad, because they are concerned only with themselves. For John Ford so-called progress —whether in the civilizing of the West after the cavalry and early settlers have tamed it, in *She Wore a Yellow Ribbon* (1949) and *The Man Who Shot Liberty Valence* (1962), or in the industrialization of a Welsh mining town in *How Green Was My Valley*, or in the new political order in *The Last Hurrah* (1958)—only corrupts the best qualities of human character.

In his most famous Western, *Stagecoach* (1939), this conflict is made clear. The values of the old West are represented by Ringo, again played by John Wayne, a simple, good-humored, honest young man intent on avenging the murder of his brother. His more sophisticated fellow passengers in the wilderness are people who exploit others—a gambler, a whiskey salesman, and a fleeing bank manager who has stolen his town's savings. The test comes, typically, when the stagecoach is attacked by Indians in the desolate wastes of the New Mexico desert. The social parasites have lost their moral fiber, and with it their courage and sense of mutual responsibility. The group is saved by Ringo, an accused murderer; Doc Boone, a drunkard; Dallas, a prostitute; and Curly, a rough professional lawman—characters who would be shunned in more refined Eastern society. Private vices are not as socially destructive as crimes that hurt others. Acquisitiveness sets people apart; sacrifice brings them together.

Ford heroes are always those who sacrifice themselves for others, for the good of the group, and thereby serve as an example for others. The crisis in *Young Mr. Lincoln* (1939) comes when Lincoln must decide, after the death of Ann Rutledge, whether to settle for a comfortable law practice in Illinois or devote his life to the painful uncertainties of national service. His figure, silhouetted on a hilltop at the end of the film, is Ford's recurrent visual sign that he is now alone and will die. In *The Grapes of Wrath*, Tom Joad's figure is outlined against the sky as he leaves family and friends to pursue a dream of social reform that will inevitably lead to persecution and death.

Ford does not glorify war and death, but he does celebrate those qualities that allow his characters to retain their humanity in the most desperate situations. Like the novelist Joseph Conrad, he investigates the beliefs and customs that support people separated from the usual socializing institutions.

Even Colonel Thursday in *Fort Apache* becomes a hero when, after refusing to escape, he rejoins his men and shares their fate. Talking to reporters after the event—Thursday's Charge, based on Custer's Last Stand—Captain York does not contradict their assumption that Thursday was a great man. According to Ford's concept of history, society needs heroes to admire and imitate, even if they were not in fact heroic. As he himself has said, "We've had a lot of people who were supposed to be great heroes, and you know damn well they weren't. But it's good for the country to have heroes to look up to." The most famous statement of this idea is the comment of the newspaper editor in *The Man Who Shot Liberty Valence* when he discovers that Ransom Stoddard, now a United States senator and local hero, did not really shoot the outlaw Liberty Valence. "When the legend becomes a fact," he says, "print the legend."

John Ford, in his many films, has chronicled the history of the United States—the frontier, the Civil War, Lincoln, the Depression, both World Wars, modern American politics—more as legend than fact. He creates history as it is remembered, as we need it to be. Yet his films are realistic in his portrayal of human character. It is a matter of emphasis. He doesn't take an individual man and show him as a hero, but takes a hero and shows him as a man. It is the difference between films like De Sica's *The Bicycle Thief* and *Umberto D* or Kurosawa's *Ikiru*, which affirm the value of ordinary human experience by refusing to dramatize it, and films like *Young Mr. Lincoln* and *They Were Expendable*, which provide us with examples of character and action we can emulate. Foreign films frequently present a human situation and allow us to draw conclusions from it, while American films usually start with a premise and illustrate it through plot and characterization.

In this, Ford is an American director. He is a moralist, and his films always make a point: That the family is a powerful force in preserving society and must be defended at all costs. That obedience to authority figures, whether the fathers of *My Darling Clementine* (1946) and *How Green Was My Valley,* or the officers in the cavalry, army, and navy films, is essential for the stable ordering of society. That human beings are defined by their will to overcome all obstacles, and it is that commitment rather than the success or failure of their effort which gives them value. That the small customs and rituals, developed over generations, are important to bind men together. That rough humor, dancing, liquor, physical activity (though not competition), and the occasional fist fight provide safe outlets for personal and group frustration. That money corrupts above all, and one's attitude toward money tells us what one is. John Ford brings a consistent view of life to his films, and he utilizes gesture as well as plot and dialogue to illustrate it.

Ford also uses nature in a strongly symbolic way. The elements reflect a character's inner state, embody a moral conflict, and communicate mood on a nonverbal level. The most complex use of nature as symbol is in the many Westerns filmed in Monument Valley, a magnificently theatrical landscape that lies within the Navajo Indian reservation in Arizona and Utah. It is a stark, parched land. Above the valley's flat, sandy plains sheer red cliffs of stone tower into a brilliant blue sky. The sun burns harsh and implacable, and massive white clouds drift imperiously overhead. It is an elemental landscape, stripped of any shelter, basic, hard, demanding energy and ingenuity to survive in.

For John Ford this harsh land forces on its inhabitants a moral way of life. Community is essential to existence. All personal differences must be submerged or settled according to custom, because disruption of the group means extinction for everyone. The land imposes on men and women a stern humility. They must respect the laws of nature and the laws of society. Survival depends on the accurate reading of natural signs—dust, wind, rain—and of human signs in their fellows. It is a classic confrontation between human society and destructive forces. The enemy can be famine and thirst or, equally dangerous, the outlaw and the Indian. Amid this basic conflict simple virtues prevail—courage, duty, honor, mutual respect. The battles that take place are played out against the backdrop of timeless formations, hard physical reality. It is a place of fact, not imagination. Of action, not words. It is a place, like the sea, or any battlefield, where humans are fragile and exposed, and what they do is what they are, without excuse or a second chance.

Ford's film technique derives from this vision of the world. He keeps dialogue to a minimum, preferring to show character through gesture and movement. At the beginning of *The Searchers* Martha Edwards goes inside to get her brother-in-law's coat and stands for a moment holding it. Another man, Clayton, sits in the next room watching her. From the way she caresses the coat, we know she secretly loves him, and from his expression we know that he is aware of it. He quietly gets up and leaves, not wanting her to realize what he has seen. It is clear he will never mention it. Not a word has been spoken, but we immediately know the relationship of these three people, what their values are, the exact way in which they repress their feelings out of respect for each other. It is a brilliant example of purely visual expression. In *Pilgrimage* (1933) a mother who has just heard of her son's death in war sits down at her desk and slowly puts together the fragments of a photograph of him she had once torn in anger. It is enough. We need know nothing more. Without comment Ford has managed to communicate more than an idea; he gives us at a deeper level an unforgettable sense of her sorrow.

Perhaps the film that most clearly illustrates Ford's use of symbolic image is *The Informer*, the story of an inarticulate man who cannot verbally express his guilt and self-revulsion. In place of dialogue Ford must make the external world represent the hidden dimensions of the man's soul. Dudley Nichols, the screenwriter and a frequent collaborator on Ford films, describes how they translated dumb emotion into cinematic terms.

> *The whole action was to be played out on one foggy night, for the fog was symbolic of the groping primitive mind; it is really a mental fog in which he moves and dies. A poster offering a reward for information concerning Gypo's friend became the symbol of the evil idea of betrayal, and it blows along the street, following Gypo; it will not leave him alone. It catches on his leg and he kicks it off. But still it follows him, and he sees it like a phantom in the air when he unexpectedly comes upon his fugitive friend. . . . The informer encounters a blind man in the dark fog outside and grips his throat in sudden guilt. The blind man is a symbol of the brute conscience, and Gypo releases him when he discovers the man cannot see. But as Gypo goes on to drown his conscience in drink, the tapping of the blind man's cane follows him; we hear it without seeing the blind man as Gypo hears his guilt pursuing him in his own soul. Later, when he comes face to face with his conscience for a terrifying moment, he tries to buy it off —by giving the blind man a couple of pounds, a lordly sum (quoted in Richard Dyer Mac Cann, Film: A Montage of Theories [New York: Dutton, 1966]).*

Viewed today, *The Informer* seems heavy-handed and obvious. But it presents us with a textbook on the method that Ford was to refine over the decades until he became the recognized master of American cinema.

John Ford was born Sean Aloysius O'Fearna either on 1 February 1895 in Cape Elizabeth, Maine, or five years earlier in Ireland. His life has become as much a legend as his movies. He explains the change of name from the anglicized O'Feeney to Ford by telling a story about his brother Francis, who was at one time a theater stage manager. When one of the actors got drunk and failed to appear for a performance, Francis took his place, and then went on to become a famous actor, under the name Frank Ford. Sean O'Fearna in turn became John Ford.

His account of how he became a movie director is equally entertaining and questionable. He had been working as an assistant director, actor, and stunt man for his brother Francis in Hollywood in the 1910s. An important producer came to visit the studio. But it is best, as always, to let Ford himself tell the tale.

> *"Then, when Carl Laemmle visited the Universal studios from New York for the first time, they gave him a big party on the only closed stage on the lot. I was a prop boy then and doubled as bartender. The party lasted most of the night, and I slept under the bar so I could be on time for work the next morning. But when I reported, neither the director nor any of the actors were there—they'd been up all night. Some of the cowboy extras were there and nobody else. Isador Bernstein, who was the General Manager then and a very wonderful person, got very upset when he saw the situation. 'The Boss is coming,' he said. 'We've got to do something.' I said, 'What?' 'Anything,' he said. So when Mr. Laemmle and his party came, I told the cowboys to go down to the end of the street and ride back toward the camera fast, yelling like hell. Laemmle seemed to like that, so Mr. Bernstein said, 'Try and do something else.' 'Well,'*

I said, 'all I can do is have 'em ride back.' He says, 'Well, do that.' So I told the cowboys, 'When I fire a shot, I want several of you guys to fall off your horses.' Now there were a lot of pretty girls in Mr. Laemmle's party, so when I fired a shot, every damn cowboy fell off his horse—showing off, you see. 'Can't you do something else?' said Bernstein. So we burned the street down. They came riding back and forth—it was more like a pogrom than a Western. Months later, Mr. Laemmle said, 'Give Jack Ford the job—he yells good' " (Peter Bogdanovich, John Ford *[Berkeley: University of California Press, 1961]).*

The film was *Straight Shooting,* a silent Western starring Harry Carey, made in 1917; it was the first of Ford's 112 feature films and over 40 short subjects, the most any director has ever made. Until his death in 1973, John Ford insisted with deceptive modesty that making movies was simply a job. He refused to admit that he had created art or that his films were important. But, one suspects, he knew better. He was a historian. He probably would have preferred to be remembered that way.

Orson Welles

Left: in the opening scene of Mr. Arkadin (1962), the dying
Bracco (Gregoire Aslan) leaves a message with the hero's girl
friend, Mily (Patricia Medina). This event will set in motion the
exposure of the mysterious Arkadin. Above: soon after revealing
Arkadin's secret past, Mily is killed. Peter Van Eyck is seated at
the right.

☆ 35

The public Kane (Orson Welles) shown after his first marriage to Emily Norton (Ruth Warrick), the niece of the President. From Citizen Kane (1941). *Right: Susan Alexander (Dorothy Comingore) is just one more object for Kane's collection. Over: each element in* Citizen Kane *was meant to comment on other elements in the shot.*

☆ 36

When asked by an interviewer in 1967 which directors he most admired, Orson Welles answered that he liked "the old masters. By which I mean John Ford, John Ford, and John Ford. With Ford at his best, you feel that the movie has lived and breathed in the real world." Previously he had said, "John Ford was my teacher. My own style has nothing to do with his, but *Stagecoach* was my movie textbook. I ran it over forty times." Whatever he learned about film construction and camera technique, Welles's subject and his treatment of it are almost diametrically opposed to Ford's. If Ford creates and preserves legends in his films, Welles explores and exposes them. Ford is clear and direct, telling a simple story simply. Welles is indirect and subtle, leading us through a labyrinth to the heart of his mystery.

Welles's hero is a man with a terrible secret that he tries to hide from others and from himself by living a lie. After a while he becomes a prisoner of that lie, and when he is finally forced to face the truth, he is shattered and dies. In a desperate attempt to maintain the deception, he tries to control his world, through power or money or murder, and when he cannot, when the facts overwhelm his self-delusion, he is destroyed. His efforts bring their own defeat, because they are based on a fatal flaw—deception of himself. No matter how many people he sacrifices, how many masks he wears, ultimately the truth of what he is causes his downfall.

In every Welles film there is someone who exposes him, who shows that the legend is hollow. Jerry Thompson, the reporter in *Citizen Kane* (1941), is assigned to uncover the facts behind the myth Charles Kane has created about himself. In *The Stranger* (1946) Inspector Wilson tracks down the ex-Nazi, Franz Kindler, who has been posing as a professor in a New England college. The young sailor, Michael O'Hara, discovers the horrible truth about the Bannisters in *The Lady From Shanghai* (1947). In *Mr. Arkadin* (1962) Van Stratten is actually hired by the powerful and mysterious Gregory Arkadin to unearth his past life so that he may suppress and obliterate it. Mike Vargas, a Mexican narcotics agent, exposes the corrupt detective Quinlan in *Touch of Evil* (1958). The Advocate in *The Trial* (1962), Virginia in *The Immortal Story* (1968), Iago in Welles's *Othello* (1955), and his Falstaff in *Chimes at Midnight* (1967) all expose their adversaries for what they really are. In *The Magnificent Ambersons* (1942) and *Macbeth* (1950), the world itself, through its ordinary, law-abiding citizens, destroys those who arrogantly refuse to live on its terms.

Welles's characters are divided between the predators—those people who destructively insist on fulfilling themselves—and the victims who have no such ambition. In *Mr. Arkadin* the main character, Gregory Arkadin, tells a story.

> *And now I'm going to tell you about a scorpion. A scorpion wanted to cross a river, so he asked a frog to carry him. "No," said the frog. "No, thank you. If I let you on my back you may sting me and the sting of the scorpion means death." "Now where," asked the scorpion, "is the logic of that? No scorpion could be judged illogical. If I sting you, you will die—I will drown." The frog was convinced and allowed the scorpion on his back but just in the middle of the river he felt a terrible pain and realized that after all the scorpion had stung him. "Logic!" cried the dying frog, as he started under, bearing the scorpion down with him. "There can be no logic in this!" "I know," said the scorpion, "but I can't help it—it's my character."*

Charles Kane, Gregory Arkadin, Hank Quinlan, and the other scorpions poison those around them and corrupt their lives. In their frantic effort to be extraordinary, they make their own laws and use people however they can. Ironically, though, we are made to feel more deeply for them than for their victims. They want to be logical, to live happily in the world like everyone else, but they can't. Their character prevents them. In a way, it's not their fault. They destroy themselves and bring others down with them because they can only be what they are. And what we come to realize is that they suffer more than anyone else. Having to be exceptional gives them no joy and only hastens their end, torturing them every step of the way.

The innocent, decent people who finally unmask them are cold and detached. They have no emotional understanding of the men they help to defeat. Welles meant it that way. "I don't detest them," he has said of the scorpions. "I detest the way they act—that is my point of tension. . . . I have sympathy for these characters—humanly, but not morally." Morally, Vargas and O'Hara and Wilson are right, but we don't like them. They are too smug and self-satisfied. They accept the world as it is because they don't have enough imagination to conceive of anything else. The predators are far more interesting. For Welles it is the difference between logic and character. Although logic eventually wins—justice is always done—it is character that fascinates him. As he said of *Mr. Arkadin*, "The point of the story is to show that a man who declares himself in the face of the world, I am as I am, take it or leave it, that this man has a sort of tragic dignity." This tragic dignity, however repulsive it may become, is the subject of his films.

Welles himself, being the kind of man he was, burst on Hollywood like a bombshell in 1939 at the age of twenty-three. Hailed as a boy genius, he had become nationally famous through his *War of the Worlds* radio broadcast, which had terrified millions of people into thinking the Martians had landed. He had been directing and acting in plays and radio dramas professionally since he was sixteen, and RKO pictures called him to Hollywood to save their ailing company. He was given total control of the pictures he made and was allowed to use his own acting company, the Mercury Theater Company he brought with him from New York.

In 1941, at the age of twenty-five, he made *Citizen Kane*. A year later he made *The Magnificent Ambersons*. A few months later he was thrown out of Hollywood. *Citizen Kane*, the film that many people consider the greatest talking picture ever made in America, stirred up the greatest controversy in the history of Hollywood. *The Magnificent Ambersons*, although dreadfully cut behind his back, and with scenes inserted that were directed by someone else, is considered almost its equal. It was a box-office failure. Welles has spent the rest of his life making low-budget films financed primarily by his own acting, and has made only a few more pictures, under severe handicaps, for Hollywood producers.

Citizen Kane, with a script by Herman J. Mankiewicz and Orson Welles, was loosely based on the life of William Randolph Hearst, this century's most powerful newspaperman. Even before the film came out, the controversy began. Hearst threatened to sue RKO and punish the film industry in his papers if the picture was released. The head of production at MGM, Louis B. Mayer, representing both Hearst and some of the more fearful film companies, offered $842,000—more than the film had cost—if all negatives and copies of the picture were burned. After it was released, most theaters refused to show it, and Hearst ordered his papers not to publicize or review any films made by RKO. It was an appropriate beginning for a movie that was to revolutionize film-making. Even today, long after the furor has died down, it is as radical as it was then. With the possible exception of John Ford, Welles has had more influence on subsequent generations of film-makers, both in the United States and abroad, than any other director.

Citizen Kane is about a man who became a legend. The question is: How much, if any, of the legend is true? And how does one find out? The film is presented in a "prismatic" style. Charles Kane's character is reflected in many mirrors, from many different points of view. The film opens with the actual scene of his death and then jumps abruptly to a newsreel account of his life. A title in the newsreel proclaims that "few private lives were more public," an assertion we for the moment accept, as we do the events presented. But suddenly the news film flicks off, a light comes on, and we are thrown into another world, seemingly more real. The editor of the newsreel and his reporters have been viewing the film. The editor, Rawlston, isn't satisfied. As he says: "It isn't enough to tell us what a man did. You've got to tell who he was." So he assigns Thompson to find out the real truth behind the glorified documentary facts of Kane's life. With Kane dead there is only one way to do that. Interview the people who knew him. For the rest of the film we accompany Jerry Thompson, his face always in shadow, on his search for the truth. But there is no truth, or there are many contradictory versions of it, and when *Citizen Kane* ends, as did the newsreel within it, we realize that the film is only a partial reality. We are left with a sense of mystery about Kane and about human nature itself.

The audience, however, knows one answer that no one in the film does. On his deathbed Kane pronounced the word "Rosebud." In all his interviews with Kane's business partners, Leland and Bernstein, with his guardian Thatcher, his mistress Susan Alexander, and his butler Raymond, Thompson never discovers the meaning of that word. In the final frames we do. It is the name of the sled that we saw taken from young Kane when he was given up by his parents. At the end Thompson is told that if he had found Rosebud, it would have explained everything about Kane's life. Thompson replies: "No, I don't think so. No. Mr. Kane was a man who got everything he wanted, and then lost it. Maybe Rosebud was something he couldn't get or something he lost. Anyway, it wouldn't have explained anything. I don't think any word can explain a man's life. No, I guess Rosebud is just a piece in a jigsaw puzzle, a missing piece." We know what Rosebud means. It represented to Kane his lost childhood, the last time he thought he was happy. It was at the moment when he lost his sled that his future was determined, that all other alternatives were canceled. But even knowing that, we don't know any more about him than Thompson does. We are left with all the facts and without the truth. Ultimately, Welles seems to be saying, *Citizen Kane* the movie, like Charles Kane the character, leaves us no more or less confused than life itself.

The techniques of *Citizen Kane* were not original, but they had never been used as boldly and ingeniously before. Deep-focus photography—adjusting the camera lens so that everything in a shot, both foreground and background, is sharply in focus—had been used as early as the 1920s, by D. W. Griffith and others. But no one had dared employ this complicated method for an entire film. Welles saw its advantages at once.

The director is given greater scope, since everything that is shown is equally clear. The audience can participate more freely in the scene, since the camera doesn't restrict their attention to selected areas of the screen. Each element in the shot can be made to comment on the others. In an early scene, when Mrs. Kane is giving her son to his future guardian, the camera simultaneously shows the relationship of all the people involved. The determined mother, the strongest figure in the group, is seen in close-up, while Thatcher sits impassively behind her, their matching profiles signaling stolid agreement. The father stands gesturing foolishly in the middle distance, isolated in the room. Behind them, seen clearly through the window, the young Kane plays in the snow, oblivious that his fate is being decided inside. His powerlessness and trust, their discord, the working of adult forces that ignore his existence are all registered in a single deep-focus shot.

This process also allows the "mise-en-scène"—the setting and atmosphere of a scene—to reflect on the characters. Kane is frequently seen in the hollow, echoing rooms of his mansion, every statue and tapestry and marble ornament as coldly and clearly defined in wide space as the man himself—a lonely figure overwhelmed by his cheerless possessions. The film contains hundreds of examples of this deep-focus process. Another occurs in the scene in which Kane visits Susan Alexander in her bedroom before she leaves her husband. Sharply focused in the foreground throughout the scene is a stuffed doll seen in profile. It indicates what Susan really is to Kane, a pretty plaything. A more experienced director would have been too intimidated by the continual difficulties of this technique to use it so often. But Welles, never having made a film before, saw no reason not to use it as much as he liked.

Welles unabashedly pushed other familiar devices to new extremes. He does not use cuts unobtrusively to get from one shot to another, but conspicuously employs them to contrast or link two scenes. The opening scene of Kane's death, shown in soft focus, is jarringly cut to the harsh melodrama of the newsreel. The private and public worlds are violently juxtaposed.

In an interview with Raymond, the butler's impersonal account of how Susan left Kane is abruptly cut to the moment itself, a parakeet screaming as she walks away. The shock to the audience is as great as to Kane, and they are prepared for the violent scene that follows.

Where previous directors used a single dissolve—the merging of one scene into another—Welles uses a rapid series of them to create a dizzying effect of movement through time and space. Like others before him, he links succeeding scenes with overlapping dialogue or sounds, but he takes the device a step further by beginning a sentence or sound in one time and place and finishing it in the next scene years later with a different person.

With the help of the brilliant musical director, Bernard Herrmann, who had never worked on a film before, Welles expands the use of music to build and structure his film. The same musical phrases will recur at seemingly unrelated moments, tying the scenes together. Or be subtly changed each time they appear anew. A melody such as the "What is his name?" tune is sung vigorously at the *Inquirer* party, is heard again played more aggressively at the political rally, becomes sadder after the election defeat, and reappears behind the credits. The breakfast scene between Kane and Emily was cut to correspond to the music, Welles patterning the montage of shots—one shot successively superimposed on and then replacing another—to follow the movement of what Herrmann called his "ballet suite." Music had seldom been used so cleverly or given such an important role in a film before.

More than the specific elements of the movie—its "film grammar"—it is the overall design of *Citizen Kane*—its "film syntax"—that marked its creator's genius. Flashbacks had been used since the beginning of films to help tell a story, but never so consistently. Again Welles took a traditional device and used it to the limit. *Citizen Kane*, in fact, is almost nothing but flashbacks. They are the mirrors that reflect Kane's increasingly distorted image back and forth to the point of infinity. As Welles describes the technique: "Each major flashback begins at a later point in time than its predecessor, but each flashback overlaps with at least one of the others, so that the same event or period is seen from two or three points of view." It is a marvellously economical method of storytelling. Not only do we get five different views of Kane, but we also get cross-views of each of the narrators and, through their own biased descriptions of each other, an insight into each of them as well.

The whole is kept tightly under control by the initial chronological presentation of Kane's life in the newsreel and by a counterpoint of images and scenes throughout the movie. It opens and closes with a shot of the "No Trespassing" sign outside Kane's mansion, a symbol that changes meaning as the film develops. There are many such repeated motifs. Another is the neon sign that flashes "Susan Alexander—Cabaret" when Thompson arrives in Atlantic City, and that is again seen later in the film, after Susan's decline, this time turned off. There is the glass paperweight with the snow scene inside that appears repeatedly throughout the movie until it falls from Kane's hand when he dies, final symbol of the life that has escaped him. And there is the sled, seen by most of the characters without their recognizing its significance, until it goes up in flames at the end, a last, futile clue to Charles Kane's unhappiness.

The major criticism of *Citizen Kane* is that its technique is too flamboyant; it calls too much attention to itself. And that the camera distances us too greatly from the living characters. But that was Welles's artistic point. He doesn't want us to get so involved with his story that we forget we are watching a movie. The meaning of the movie derives from its relationship, as an artificially constructed form, to our own reality. We can't identify with Thompson, because he is never more than a shadowy figure probing a mystery. We can't identify with Kane, because he exists in so many guises that we get no unified sense of him. The other characters seem to be simply figures of Kane's and Welles's imagination. We are left with the movie itself, which is no more than a point of view. The techniques of the film *are* the film, as our perception of reality, unsupported by any absolute knowledge, is in fact our only reality.

François Truffaut, the French film director, has said of Welles's second movie, *The Magnificent Ambersons,* "This film was made in violent contrast to *Citizen Kane,* almost as if by another film-maker who detested the first and wanted to give him a lesson in modesty." Where the style of *Citizen Kane* is brash and energetic, a dazzling display of directorial virtuosity, *The Magnificent Ambersons* is deceptively simple and subdued. Welles has gone from concentration on the cut to the scene itself. Shifts of scene in the first movie are emphasized for maximum effect, while in the second, transitions are disguised through imperceptible dissolves. The difference in style is dictated by the difference in subject. *Citizen Kane* deals with the frenetic, disorganized life of a newspaper tycoon. It is a movie of action. *The Magnificent Ambersons* treats the end of a leisurely era and the collapse of a family. It is a film of mood and character. The first is a violent attack on a ruthless, immoral man. The second is a memorial to another, more civilized way of life. As Welles commented, this film is a lament "not so much for the epoch as for the sense of moral values which are destroyed."

This sense of nostalgia for the late nineteenth century is evoked at the beginning of the film through a series of scenes framed in soft focus, like antique postcards of the period. Much like the newsreel in *Citizen Kane,* this device serves many purposes; the opening series of scenes quickly summarizes the first seventeen years of George Amberson's life. Through voice-over narration, sound effects, and music, it also shows the evolution of the period, connecting the growing up of a boy with the development of a city and of an age in American social history. From the outset Welles suggests that the failing fortunes of the Ambersons will be associated with the growing physical ugliness and corruption of values in their time. The film begins in gaiety and light and gradually darkens somberly as the family, and what they represent, is destroyed by progress.

The spirit of the Ambersons and their world is vividly created in an early scene through Welles's handling of the camera. He employs deep-focus photography and uses the camera as a silent participant, much as he had done in the previous film. But here these techniques are used more surely and to greater effect. It is a ball to celebrate George's homecoming, and the camera, after a long shot of the house, accompanies George and Lucy Morgan inside. We pass through the doors and are immediately swept up in the excitement of the occasion. In a long, unbroken shot we circle the dance floor, eavesdrop on conversations, and watch people talking, eating, and dancing in every area of the room. Because of the extreme clarity of the photography, the textures and movement are immediate and precise. The lavish furnishings, the polished wood and patterned walls and intricately inlaid floors, the faces and clothing of the guests, the shifting shadows and highlights that cover and reveal them, all combine to give a sense of richness and settled splendor. The people, although seen as distinct individuals, are also firmly placed in their surroundings. When those surroundings are gone, the people will be lost, their unquestioned harmony shattered. In a brief ten-minute scene, Welles has created an entire world and, as we later discover, every aspect of that world will crumble and pass away.

The themes of these two early films will be repeated through Welles's later work. Techniques and symbols explored in the first movies will also be used in the last. It is almost as if the work of Orson Welles comes round full circle. In *Citizen Kane*, Charles Kane drops a glass ball, representing lost innocence, when he dies. In *The Immortal Story*, made almost thirty years later, the dying Mr. Clay drops a seashell to the floor, emblematic of the natural life he never lived. Even comments made about the later characters tell us more about the earlier ones. In *Citizen Kane*, Thompson comments that "Mr. Kane was a man who got everything he wanted and then lost it." Levinsky, in *The Immortal Story*, says of Clay after his death, "It's very hard on people who want things so badly that they can't do without them. If they can't get the things it's hard. And when they do get them, surely it is very hard." That observation can stand equally for every Welles hero and, perhaps, for Welles himself.

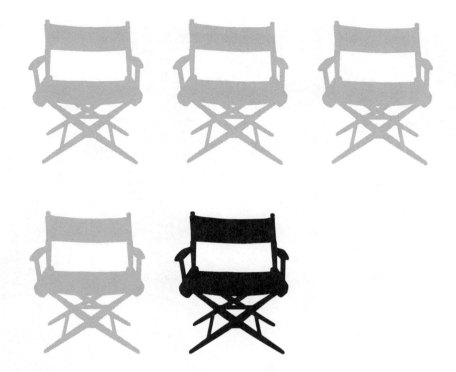

Howard
Hawks

Above: in Only Angels Have Wings (1939) *the separation of characters from each other in a single frame indicates the degree of involvement and acceptance. From left to right, Jeff Carter (Cary Grant), Bonnie Lee (Jean Arthur), Les Peters (Allyn Joslyn), and Dutchman (Sig Ruman). Right: Bat McPherson (Richard Barthelmess, dressed in tie and suit), resented by the other pilots, is isolated from the group until he redeems himself.*

☆ 50

☆ 51

Hawks keeps his lens at eye-level, as in this scene, above, from Red River *(1948). The plan is to evoke the intensity of a particularly dramatic moment. Hawks believes that only through the disciplined acceptance of personal responsibility can we find the freedom to love and keep the world from going mad. Montgomery Clift finally convinces John Wayne of that fact at the end of* Red River.

Working within the familiar forms—subjects his audience knows well—allows Hawks the freedom to study stereotyped characters and situations in depth. Typical are the cowboys at left from Rio Bravo (1959): John Wayne (John T. Chance) and Dean Martin (Dude). John Chance is not the typical Wayne character. He is shown as needing help and lucky to get it. Claude Akins is the man Wayne is pointing his rifle at (above).

In *Only Angels Have Wings* (1939) Jeff Carter says of a mail plane pilot who has just crashed while making a landing in the fog, "Joe died flying, didn't he? Well, that was his job. He just wasn't good enough." He also tells Bonnie Lee, when she sits down at the piano—as Sean Mercer tells Dallas in almost exactly the same scene in *Hatari!* over twenty years later—"You better be good." In typical Hawksian fashion she doesn't say anything; she plays. She proves that she is. In *The Big Sleep* (1946) Philip Marlowe, played by Humphrey Bogart, pays the supreme compliment to Vivian, played by Lauren Bacall, when he says, "You're good, you're very good." It is a sign of respect, acceptance, and love. It is the statement of an attitude that recurs throughout Hawks's long film career. As early as 1932 Cesca in *Scarface* asks her brother, "I'm just like you Tony, aren't I? I'm not afraid," as they are about to be shot down by the police. The fact that she is with him is proof enough. As late as *Rio Lobo* in 1971 Jorge Rivero must show, in the face of strong mistrust, that he is good enough to help the always competent John Wayne.

Being good is a quality of character as well as ability, and the two are closely related. The Hawks hero is a professional who defines himself through his job—how dedicated he is to it and how much he will sacrifice for it. He accepts total responsibility for what he does, without excuses, and performs it unobtrusively, with courage, endurance, and a complete lack of self-pity. The two sins are sentimentality and loss of self-control. Sentimentality shows an excess of emotion when action is needed. It also suggests that you can't accept the world as it is but must soften it with false feeling. Loss of self-control—whether cowardice (Bat McPherson is shunned for bailing out of a plane in which his friend died in *Only Angels Have Wings*) or ambition and greed (Ned Arp endangers other drivers by continuing his career with a mutilated hand in *Red Line 7000*) or self-indulgence (Harry Morgan says of the drunken Eddie in *To Have and Have Not* that "he used to be good")—is a personal weakness and prevents self-respect. Self-respect is all-important for the Hawks hero. It allows him to act confidently on impulse and instinct, and gives him the maturity and strength of character to lead others less self-reliant than himself.

Like many of his characters, Howard Hawks is good, but not obviously so and not according to the usual standards. He is one of the last American directors to be considered a major artist. To some extent this is because, like those characters in his films who naturally discount their achievements, he refuses to claim his work is anything but entertainment. He has defined the good director merely as "somebody who doesn't annoy you," and has continually insisted, "I'm interested in having people go and see the picture, and enjoy it." His films are so enjoyable that they have been dismissed as superficial.

Other things have worked against his reputation. He has always chosen to work within the standard Hollywood genres, making traditional Westerns, hard-boiled gangster movies, zany situation comedies, and exciting adventure films. He has never made a serious film on an important subject or produced a single generally acclaimed classic like Welles's *Citizen Kane* or Ford's *Stagecoach*. He does not make obviously sociological documents like Stanley Kramer and Sidney Lumet or psychological dramas like William Wyler and Elia Kazan. Finally, his film technique hasn't brought him much praise because it is so simple and straightforward. In fact until recently his work hadn't been highly regarded, because his forty-one feature films, made in a career spanning almost half a century, have never sought to call attention to their style, their intellectual content, or to the man who made them.

The surface of a Hawks film is deceptively smooth and uncomplicated. Action, gestures, and dialogue strike us so immediately and directly that we get their meaning without being aware of it. Hawks plunges us into his story as quickly as possible and keeps the momentum going with a minimum of technical intrusion. The camerawork is clean, spare, and economical.

There is little camera movement to distract us from the actors and the action. Hawks seems to find exactly the right camera setup—where he places his camera—for each scene, and unless there is a good reason for moving it, he leaves it there. When he does use a moving camera, it is integrally related to the action, and because it is done so infrequently, it serves as a kind of punctuation. In *The Big Sleep* Marlowe is questioning Joe Brody, a gambler and blackmailer. As Brody tells one lie after another, he turns in his chair to avoid looking at Marlowe, and the detective steadily circles him to watch his eyes. The camera moves slowly around them, setting up a third circle, and the effect is ominous. It emphasizes Brody's defenselessness and makes a distanced, contemptuous comment on his pathetic dishonesty. It keeps him coldly on the spot, and we are not surprised, shortly afterward, that he is killed.

Unlike Hitchcock, Hawks doesn't use montage. He prefers to shoot scenes in one long take without disturbing our attention with disruptive cuts. There are few "reaction shots"—a technique for creating tension. In a reaction shot, if two people are talking, the camera will cut back and forth to record the reaction of the listener; or if a door opens while the camera is on one of the characters, the camera will give us that character's reaction before it shifts to the person who has entered. Hawks would rather keep all action in the same frame by using long shots. The relationship between characters interests him more than the individual. In *Rio Bravo* (1959) Dude, Stumpy, and Colorado, the three flawed characters, sit in a close group in the jail singing. Chance, the man who saved them and brought them together, making this scene possible, stands apart from it. Both from the look on his face and from his physical position in the frame, we understand his complex attitude toward them.

In *Only Angels Have Wings* the separation of characters from each other in a single frame indicates the degree of involvement and acceptance. Bat McPherson, resented by the other pilots, is isolated from the group until he redeems himself. Bonnie Lee, an outsider, remains physically in the background until she is initiated into their close-knit community. Besides keeping his figures within the frame, Hawks usually keeps their entire bodies within the shot, thus relating each gesture to the person making it. Rather than forcing our attention on a face or hand or object, he continually relates the character to the surroundings and the other people in the scene, making us forget that a selective camera is at work.

For the same reason, there are few close-ups in Hawks's films, and those only when absolutely necessary. A close-up usually creates a psychological effect through facial expression, whereas Hawks prefers to indicate emotion and thought through gesture and action. A characteristic scene occurs in *Rio Bravo* when Dude stands across the street and watches Sheriff Chance force a hired gunman away from the jail by the tone of his voice in saying "Good evening." We see Dude's face register his expression of awe and admiration for the man and the act. We see what has caused his reaction—ourselves responding as he does—and at the same time we get a complete sense of the essential personalities of the two antagonists. Without pans or cuts or close-ups Hawks has given us the entire situation in a single shot in a single instant.

Maintaining this sense of the camera as a natural, unobtrusive instrument, Hawks keeps his lens at eye-level—the angle from which we ordinarily see things. Unlike Orson Welles, there are very few crane shots from above or low-angle shots from below, no trick camera shots through the scenery or from a character's peculiar point of view. When there is an unusually dramatic shot—the spectacular panorama of the cattle drive at dawn in *Red River* (1948), or the view from the wagons of the river crossing later in the film—it is to evoke the intensity of a particularly dramatic moment. Similarly, there are no flashbacks in Hawks's films. He wants to keep the action moving forward at all times, absorbing the viewer into the natural flow of events without confusion or distraction.

Like his uncluttered camerawork, Hawks's dialogue is kept to a minimum and is always terse and to the point. He prefers to let actions speak for themselves. As he has said: "We have a scene that we're going to do; I'm interested first in the action and next in the words they speak. If I can't make the action good, I don't try to use the words." Our first view of Tony Camonte, the gangland killer in *Scarface*, is of a slowly looming, hunched, apelike shadow on the wall. He silently stalks his victim. Nothing he could possibly say would reveal this primitive, mindless being more effectively than this silent pursuit. The opening minutes of *Rio Bravo* establish the relationship of the characters and the moral theme of the film without a word being spoken—Dude's groveling for a coin in the spittoon, Chance's look of disappointment and contempt before he stops him, Dude's striking him for interfering, Dude's beating by Burdett, Chance's helping him once again, and Dude's final impulsive reaction in saving his life.

The cigarette scene at the beginning of *Only Angels Have Wings* is a classic of nonverbal thematic expression. Jeff Carter, the strong, independent crew chief, is introduced giving flight instructions to Joe Souther. He takes out a cigarette, strikes his last match, which breaks, and distractedly looks around for another. He is obviously used to someone supplying one. When he sees that Bonnie Lee, whom he hasn't met, is smoking a cigarette, he unthinkingly takes it from her, lights his own, and then continues talking to Souther with the forgotten cigarette still in his hand. As Bonnie, unnoticed, tries to retrieve it, his hand continually jerks away, and she is forced to chase after it, finally grabbing it and giving him a disgusted look. The exchange perfectly illustrates what their relationship is to be. Later the closeness between Carter and his friend Kid Dabb is suggested when Kid rolls a cigarette and without looking up, Jeff reaches for it precisely the second it's finished. In the same way, the former intimacy between Jeff and Judy is shown when he reaches for a cigarette and she automatically lights a match at the same time.

When dialogue is used, it is in conjunction with action and subservient to it. Immediately after Joe Souther's death the other pilots sit down to dinner. Bonnie, newly arrived and unfamiliar with their customs, is shocked at their apparent callousness. The steaks are served and Jeff takes Joe's. Bonnie is appalled and asks him if he really plans to eat it. "What do you want me to do," Jeff asks her, "have it stuffed?" Bonnie insists that it was Joe's. Two words and the action that goes with them give us an entire moral philosophy. "Who's Joe?" he asks, determinedly digging into the steak.

Virtually the same line repeated in three different films can take on three different meanings according to character and context. Jeff Carter's painful understatement as he gathers up Kid Dabb's belongings after his death—"Not much to show for twenty years' flying"—is a grimly restrained expression of loss, a doubt of whether such sacrifice is worth it, and an acceptance that when he dies there won't be much to show either. In *Air Force* (1943) the crew chief receives the belongings of his son, who has been killed in the war. His comment, "Not much to show for twenty years," refers not to his son's chosen profession but to his entire life. For both men it is personal, but in a different way. In *Red River*, Tom Dunson stands over the grave of a man he has killed and says, "We brought nothing into this world, and it's certain we can take nothing out." It has become an ironic philosophic statement, made more in resignation than in sorrow, given the fact that he has dedicated his life to becoming rich and powerful.

In the same way that Hawks's technique is strictly functional and his dialogue purposely undramatic, his choice of subject is always modest. All of his work has been in the "bread and butter" movies, which are guaranteed box-office successes because they have been made profitably so many times before. He has come to each genre rather late, making his films after others have established the field. This has made his contribution seem just another unoriginal, if competent, formula film. But again he is deceptive. Being a good workman, he has made one of the best, and frequently *the* best, movie in each category. And beneath the conventional surface of his films is the less obvious statement of serious moral themes. Working within the familiar forms—subjects his audiences know by heart—allows him the freedom to study these stereotyped characters and situations in depth.

Rio Bravo, a typical Western, is a case in point. All the familiar stock characters are there—the taciturn two-fisted sheriff; his undependable sidekick; the young, inexperienced kid; the girl from the saloon; the old drunk or village fool for comic relief. Hawks takes these worn clichés and turns them around, works against them. The stock characters are portrayed realistically, in terms of how things probably were.

John Chance, played by John Wayne acting against his usual image, is not the infallible lawman. In fact, though he always refuses help—for fear of getting men with families killed—he always needs it, and luckily for him it is always there. Dude is more than undependable. He is a wreck of a man, self-destructive, humiliated, without any reason to live. Feathers is not merely a pretty barroom singer; she is a strong, intelligent, independent woman who influences the hero far more than he does her. Stumpy is comic, but he is no relief. His foolishness is a carefully calculated mask to hide his fear and lack of belief in himself, qualities that he shares with the other characters. The plot is that of the hackneyed Western. The story is about five flawed people who desperately need each other without wanting to admit it, who teach each other self-reliance and self-respect, and who manage to redeem themselves with the considerable help of others. The action is moral as well as recognizably physical, and the subject is human dignity.

The Crowd Roars (1932) is more than a thrilling racing-car film with the predictably tough James Cagney. Again, the familiar clichés are reversed. In a climactic scene Cagney is knocked down by his brother without retaliating. And he is not tough. Rather, he is a miserable alcoholic who almost destroys himself because he won't leave other people alone. Within the framework of fast cars and beautiful women, Hawks fashions a story of the intricate love-hate relationship between two men, the younger fighting for maturity and independence, the older both helping and hindering him. As in many of Hawks's movies it is a woman, strong, resilient, determined, who makes them accept each other.

The central theme of *The Crowd Roars* also appears in almost every Hawks film. It always involves a group of dedicated professionals who live a dangerous, abnormal existence separate from ordinary society and who must therefore define for themselves a moral code. In *Air Force* it is the subordination of personal interests for the good of the group; in *Only Angels Have Wings* it is a fragile philosophy that permits men to face death daily; in *To Have and Have Not* it is the problem of maintaining personal integrity and freedom while also fulfilling your responsibility to others.

If responsibility and self-control are the themes of Hawks's serious dramas, irresponsibility and loss of control are the subjects of his comedies. Here the consistency of his concerns over a long career can be clearly seen. As early as *Scarface* in 1932— certainly not a comedy—the questions are introduced that will reappear in his later satires. Tony Camonte is a killer without a conscience, an unconscious savage who follows impulse and instinct. He exists on the animal level, satisfying his desires with ruthless directness. But there is also a tremendous vitality about him, a charm, an unquestioning delight with life. He is strangely innocent, without guilt or self-awareness. The result of his unrestrained self-indulgence is that he turns the world about him upside down, reversing all values, and almost destroys it as he destroys himself.

This is also the theme of the comedies. Susan, in *Bringing Up Baby*, is a less dangerous Tony. Free-spirited and irrepressible, she brings chaos into the stuffily ordered intellectual world of David Huxley. Amoral, without the slightest shred of guilt, she teaches him the joys of irresponsibility. He learns the dangers when she accidentally destroys his lifework, a painstakingly constructed dinosaur skeleton. She turns them both into children and finally reduces them to playful animals as they search for her pet leopard. Walter Burns in *His Girl Friday* is a more attractive Tony. He is an unethical predator who gets what he wants, sacrificing people and principles and leaving a trail of devastation behind him. In *Ball of Fire* (1941) the disruptive pleasures of instinct and irresponsibility again undermine the academic world as Sugarpuss O'Shea turns a group of staid professors into little boys, and brings out the beast in her timid lover. In *Monkey Business* (1952) the characters literally become children after drinking a youth-restoring drug poured into a water cooler by a monkey. Throwing off all social inhibitions, they show what they really are, savage, selfish, insensitive little beings descended from the ape. It is, at bottom, a grim, harsh view of human nature, whether presented through the delightful excesses of a Walter Burns, the studied cynicism of a Jeff Carter, or the casual fatalism of a Harry Morgan. Hawks's point, although he would deny ever having made one, is that only through the disciplined acceptance of personal responsibility can we find the freedom to love and keep our world from going mad.

**Alfred
Hitchcock**

Left: Eve Kandall (Eva Marie Saint) is one of the many Hitch-cock heroines who are not what they appear to be. In North by Northwest (1959), *she appears to be working with bad guy Mar-tin Landau. One of Hitchcock's more fascinating devices is to show a man attacked by a machine gone mad. This scene in* North by Northwest *in which Cary Grant is pursued by an air-plane is particularly frightening because the wide-open farm country looks so harmless.*

☆ 67

The major theme in Hitchcock's movies is that we are none of us what we think ourselves to be. Above: in the opening scene of Psycho (1960) we disapprove of Janet Leigh and John Gavin. Later in the film, Hitchcock will evoke conflicting emotions. Right: stopped by a policeman (Mort Mills), Janet Leigh worries that she has been reported for stealing her firm's money. We don't want her to get caught. Hitchcock is forcing us to reconsider our attitudes toward stealing.

Above: following her conversation with Norman Bates (Anthony Perkins) at the motel, Janet Leigh decides to return the money. We applaud her decision. Right: the owl acts as a symbol in Psycho. It belongs to the night world, and since Norman Bates kills at night, he feels the bird's eyes are watching him. They reinforce his own feeling of guilt. Over: in the shower that is symbolically washing away her crime and her guilt, Janet Leigh is murdered. It is partly the injustice of the killing that upsets us. She doesn't deserve to die.

Everyone remembers it. The murder of Janet Leigh in *Psycho* (1960). The image of water and blood swirling down the dark bathtub drain, the shift to the single, dead eye, and the spiraling camera movement out of the eye to a view of the body. This is "pure cinema." Melanie, trapped alone in the attic, hopelessly fighting off the last terrifying attack in *The Birds* (1963). Scottie's nightmare in *Vertigo* (1958), walking through the graveyard to Carlotta's open grave and falling forward into the pit, into unending darkness. The tennis-match scene in *Strangers on a Train* (1951), the faces of the crowd swinging back and forth in unison and only one—Bruno's—fixed frozen on his victim. These are visual images that affect us in a powerful way and yet can't be easily explained or verbally analyzed. They simply have a horrifying, unsettling impact. They stay with us for years afterward, clear, disturbing, the perfect visual trigger for our deepest emotions.

Alfred Hitchcock is one of the greatest masters of pure cinema. As he describes it, "Pure cinema is complementary pieces of film put together, like notes of music to make a melody" (quoted in Peter Bogdanovich, *The Cinema of Alfred Hitchcock* [New York: Museum of Modern Art, 1963]). Speaking of why he is writing an article on *Rear Window* (1954), he says: "I chose this picture because of all the films I have made, this to me is the most cinematic. I'm a purist so far as the cinema is concerned. You see many films that are what I call photographs of people talking. This film has as its basic structure the purely visual. The story is told only in visual terms. . . . It represents for me the purest form of cinema which is called montage: that is, pieces of film put together to make up an idea" (Alfred Hitchcock, *Take One*, November-December 1968, p. 18).

Pudovkin, the great Russian director, illustrated this method in a classic test. He filmed a close-up of an actress and placed various objects in front of her. Viewers saw her expression seem to change with each object—she appeared to look affectionately at a baby, hungrily at food, fearfully at a knife. But her expression had actually never changed. It was the relationship between the images, not the images themselves, that made the viewers think it had. This is the principle of montage. The murder scene in *Psycho*, lasting forty-five seconds, has seventy-eight cuts—seventy-eight separate pieces of film—most of them no more than two or three frames long. Taken together, they are profoundly frightening. For Hitchcock it is the essence of the motion picture. If the images are the right ones, and they are assembled in the right order, they will make the spectator not only see, but feel what the film is presenting.

An extended example of this ability to create suspense and shock through camera movement and montage is the famous chase sequence in *North by Northwest* (1959). Roger Thornhill, played by Cary Grant, is a charming, irresponsible, self-centered man easily at home in the modern world. Like many Hitchcock characters, he naively assumes that his world is a safe, dependably secure place, and that his identity is stable. His abrupt introduction to the irrational chaos that lurks beneath the appearance of things comes when he is mistaken for another man, his identity literally thrown into question, and kidnapped. Later he is told that if he meets the man he has been taken for, George Kaplan, everything will be explained. In fact he has been set up to be murdered. Hitchcock has commented that he designed this scene to avoid the usual cliché of a man lured into a dark street, positioned under a street lamp, and gunned down from a passing limousine. Instead, Grant is sent out to wide open farm country on a bright, sunny day. This is even more frightening, however, because the attack can come from anywhere and there is no place to hide. The innocence of the landscape adds tension—death simply doesn't happen in such places.

Suspense for the audience comes from both identifying with Grant—the entire scene is presented subjectively from his point of view—and from knowing more than he does about what will happen. Yet we don't know exactly where or how, which puts us closer to him than to his killers. We see Eve Kandall—one of the many Hitchcock heroines who isn't what she seems—in a phone booth, but we can't hear what she says. Although we assume she is betraying him, we also believe she loves him, so there is a chance she won't go through with it. Part of the conflict is that we both do and don't want her to. As in so many Hitchcock films, we want the horrible thing to happen—our morbid curiosity attracts us to the forbidden act—and at the same time we don't, because of our basic sympathy for the character. Also we trust Hitchcock to save Grant somehow. But with Hitchcock this is always a dangerous assumption. If we want a character killed, he often seems to be saying, he will do it for us, forcing us to become accomplices to the crime and then having to accept our own guilt. He makes us responsible for our darkest wishes by satisfying them.

The suspense of the scene begins with Grant's long wait for Kaplan. There are many false starts. He sees a car coming but it races by him. Another comes from the opposite direction —possibly this is him—and he turns to watch it go by. Then a truck appears, possibly a more likely vehicle for such a strange meeting. It throws up a cloud of dust, momentarily obscuring Grant—has he been shot?—and the camera pans to the left, away from him. There is a tense pause until he reenters the frame.

As if suggesting that the attack won't come by such an obvious route, Hitchcock has a very long shot of a car coming across the fields. Surely this must be it. The camera cuts from the expectant Grant to the car, then back to Grant. The car stops, a man gets out and waits across the road. We are as perplexed as Grant. Despite what we know, we begin to share his uninformed point of view. Grant approaches the man and, after a brief conversation, he and we are relieved. He is waiting for a bus.

But it is a false relief. Hitchcock waits until we are off

guard, attributing, as Grant does, no particular danger to the meeting or the airplane that comes into view. Then he quietly introduces the farmer's offhand remark, "That plane's dusting crops where there ain't no crops." It takes a moment for this to hit us, and before we can react, the man and his bus are gone. Grant is alone. More alone than before. But he is still oblivious. Our discomfort grows as he glances at his watch, a familiar, comfortable gesture become ominously absurd in the face of his approaching death. He is actually impatient. Then it happens. The plane, out of place as the urban, falsely assured man is out of place, attacks him. His wit and charm are no help now. It suddenly becomes man against pitiless machine—a machine gone mad—and he is reduced to what he has been all along, a vulnerable, defenseless, foolishly complacent human being.

The cutting of shots from Grant to the plane increases in speed and intensity until we, our previous faith that nothing could really happen to him gone, are also being pursued—we are running for our lives. But the extent of his helplessness hasn't been revealed yet. He sees a car coming and tries to wave it down. It ignores him. His danger is greater. He runs into the cornfield, a sure hiding place. For a moment the plane seems to be gone. When it reappears, it passes over him. He smiles to himself. He and we have outwitted them. This premature relief makes the return of the plane even more startling. This time there is no question of safety. The plane sprays poison gas and Grant is forced into the open, but not before a camera shot from Grant's point of view shows us a truck coming. It is a last hope for survival, the last-minute rescue we always expect in the movies. He runs into the road, the camera close behind him, waving it down. The sound of the plane banking a turn and the blare of the truck horn coincide; certainly the truck will arrive first. And in fact it does. The camera cuts from a close-up of Grant to the fast-approaching truck and—the impossible—the truck can't stop in time. He is run over.

Before we can register our disbelief, the plane comes in low, hits the truck, and explodes. The killer has paid. But what about the innocent men inside the truck? They leap out and run comically toward the cornfield. We have momentarily forgotten about Grant. Our tension is happily relieved by brief laughter, and then we see Grant running toward the camera, safe. When a crowd gathers to watch the burning truck, Grant backs away from them—finally taking independent action—and leaps into a parked pickup and drives away. The owner, a bow-legged farmer, runs awkwardly after him, and we can finally laugh freely. The normal, ordered world has been restored. We relax. Everything seems as safe and secure as it first appeared to be.

The world of Alfred Hitchcock is never safe. The calm, familiar, reassuring details of ordinary life merely form a thin shell over the darker forces of fear, destruction, madness, and death. It is no accident that in *Psycho* Janet Leigh is brutally murdered in the antiseptic shower of a commonplace motel. That the insane murderer in *Shadow of a Doubt* (1943) brings out the paranoiac terror of a peaceful Midwestern town and shatters the complacent world of a perfectly ordinary young girl. That the birds in *The Birds* attack children at a picnic. Or that Cary Grant almost dies in a cornfield. Bruno Anthony in *Strangers on a Train* is a most engaging young man. Norman Bates in *Psycho* is a sad, sympathetic, sensitive individual. Uncle Charlie in *Shadow of a Doubt* is a considerate, pleasant, attractive figure. But this discrepancy between appearance and reality does not apply only to the criminally insane. It exists in everyone—in Hitchcock's sane, sensible characters and his sane, sensible audience.

The major theme in the films of Alfred Hitchcock is that none of us are what we think ourselves to be. His films illustrate this by completely involving us in terror and violence, and by evoking in us conflicting reactions to his characters. The first scene in *Psycho* shows Marion and Sam meeting secretly to make love during their brief lunch break in a seedy hotel. They are unattractive characters. Then we begin to side with Marion. Sam won't marry her because he doesn't have enough money and is only after sex anyway. She doesn't care about money and really loves him. We approve of that. A short time later she is entrusted with forty thousand dollars by her boss, and she decides to steal it. As she flees, a policeman follows her, suspicious of her sleeping in the car, and we hope he won't stop her. Our attitude toward money and stealing has changed. Or rather, another contradictory attitude has emerged. Our reaction is further complicated by the fact that we don't like Sam, don't want her to marry him, which if she is successful she will do. Most importantly, her criminal act has temporarily isolated her from the moral human community and shown that, under certain circumstances, even the nicest people steal.

When she arrives at the motel, she has a long conversation with Norman Bates. As a result she decides to return the money, which we applaud, and takes a shower—symbolically washing away her crime and her guilt. Then she is murdered. It is partly the injustice of the killing that upsets us. She doesn't deserve to die—as if somehow she might have before. Crime exposes you to the danger of criminals. Her return to innocence affects our attitude toward her death, though it shouldn't. No one deserves to die.

When Norman Bates pushes Marion's car into the swamp, he tosses in the bundle of money, thinking it is a newspaper. We are appalled. Forty thousand dollars going to waste. Yet earlier we had judged Sam for thinking money so important. Hitchcock is not trying to show that we are hypocrites, but that we are both moral and immoral beings.

In a further parallel between supposedly good and bad people, Marion—a "normal" person—has momentarily given in to a compulsion to steal. She does it passively, almost as if she doesn't know what she is doing. Norman, a psychotic murderer, also gives in to his compulsion passively, and literally doesn't know what he is doing. He acts under the delusion that he is his mother. Marion acts under the influence of Sam. The two characters are more similar than they at first seem. The act of stealing draws Marion into a dark world she has no knowledge of, the world we see in the terrible extreme of Norman Bates.

This sharing of guilt—between character and character, and audience and character—is central to Hitchcock's art. The clearest example of it is found in *Strangers on a Train* when Bruno offers to exchange murders with Guy. He mentions it because Guy has suggested that his wife Miriam is in the way. She is a coarse, grasping woman who is blackmailing her husband. Guy of course doesn't take him seriously. But when Bruno does murder Miriam, his claim that Guy wanted him to do it is not completely unfounded. Guy is a moral accomplice to the crime, and by supporting his wish that she die, so are we. Guy voices the desire; Bruno acts on it. In the same way, we come to the theater with concealed desires for mayhem and murder, and Hitchcock supplies them. Bruno becomes Guy's alter ego; he acts out those destructive instincts that Guy won't admit to. Once unleashed, however, they pursue him as Bruno does, until he must accept his guilt and thus be free of it.

The degree of his, and our, absorption into Bruno's world comes when Guy goes to the Anthony house to see the father, the man Bruno wants killed. He goes late at night carrying a gun, and once upstairs, standing indecisively before the closed bedroom door, he takes the gun out and then puts it back in his pocket. Neither he nor we know what he will do with it, but there is a possibility that he will kill, if only to make Bruno leave him alone. We would not entirely object to this grisly solution, because Hitchcock has made us identify with him. Throughout the film we dreaded his possible exposure, even though he is a morally unattractive figure. He is a social climber, marrying Ann (Miriam's replacement) not for love but position, an opportunist and an emotionally dishonest man. Nevertheless we still want him to marry Ann and become successful. Our attitudes at this suspenseful moment are considerably confused.

When he enters the bedroom, it is dark. Like Marion, whatever his previous plan was, he suddenly changes his mind. He won't kill Mr. Anthony, he'll tell him about Bruno. At that second the light clicks on, and we see the figure on the bed. It is Bruno. The audience's response is shock. Partly from surprise and fear of what Bruno will now do. But also because, as he smiles, he has found us out. We are not so different from him, and if pushed far enough, we will allow what he represents to overwhelm us.

Hitchcock shows us our emotional confusion, as he has shown us our moral confusion, by continually defeating our expectations. He knows that to become involved in a film, we must identify with someone. The kind of character we readily identify with reflects our values, and the fact that we want to escape from ourselves into another identity reveals our instability. There is nothing wrong with this, he seems to suggest, but it is important to realize how easily you can be manipulated. And realize how firmly your emotional needs are rooted.

In *Psycho* we are presented with Janet Leigh, an attractive, well-known actress playing the part of a sympathetic character. We sit back, expecting to follow her fortunes through the film. A few minutes later she is murdered. The shock of the crime derives as much from our preconception of what a film should do as from the actual act. You don't kill off heroines this quickly. And you certainly don't kill off movie stars in the first fifteen minutes and leave only character actors. We are momentarily disoriented because our identity figure is gone. Don't worry, Hitchcock seems to say, I'll give you another one. So he introduces the private detective Arbogast, who, though he is first presented as an unsavory character, will at least track down Marion's killer. We can relax again. But a few minutes later he is dead. We are left with only one character to associate ourselves with, the earnest and pathetic Norman Bates. We will not believe that he is a homicidal maniac—we need him—and so continue to believe, as he does, that his mother has done the killing. When we finally see what he is, and that we have identified with him, we are not only shocked but disturbed by our misplaced trust, and thrown into emotional confusion. We want to be directed, as an audience, told what to feel about whom, and the director has betrayed us horribly.

Hitchcock explores this need for illusion most fully in *Vertigo*. Scottie, played by James Stewart, is a man who drifts without direction, who can't make up his mind about anything. He is deeply dissatisfied with the real world. He seemingly has a choice between two women. Midge is open, practical, and unexciting—a representative of life as it is. Madeleine is exotic, mysterious, complex, a perfect fantasy figure. He falls in love with Madeleine and lets her lead him into her world of drama and illusion. She becomes, for the audience as well as for him, the wish fulfillment of the dream woman. Two-thirds of the way through the movie, having strongly tied us to this character, Hitchcock betrays us—she dies suddenly and inexplicably. Even though we know that she is a fantasy within a fantasy, we are disappointed and confused. We are, surprisingly—it is only a film, after all—as disoriented as Scottie is. Soon after, Hitchcock explains what has happened, and we realize that we have been deceived, with Scottie, by a cheap trick. Neither audience nor hero wants to believe it. We both want her back. We prefer the illusion, false as it is, to the reality.

Through Scottie we are made to see and feel the consequences of rejecting real people for a dream. Judy, a graceless, uninteresting girl, has been impersonating Madeleine all along. Still obsessed with Madeleine, Scottie forces Judy to recreate her role for him. At first she resists, wanting to be loved for herself, but then, like so many of us, she agrees to conform to his image of her. Otherwise she will lose him.

Two fundamental themes in Hitchcock are explored here:

the question of personal identity, and the relationship of appearance and reality. Judy is not Madeleine, yet the qualities that Scottie loves are in Judy, otherwise she couldn't so convincingly act them. But they are not integrated in her personality, because she does not accept them as really hers, and neither does Scottie. They both reject the real girl for the fantasy. And both of them lose. Scottie, because he wants the impossible when the possible, equally fine, is standing before him. Judy, because she is a prisoner of her own creation, unable to value herself as the woman she can potentially be. Scottie has fallen in love with the appearance, and his life has become meaningless without it. Judy must maintain the appearance, because that is what he loves. When Judy dies, taking both appearance and reality with her, Scottie is thrown back on the real world. He must accept it. He no longer has a choice. And this acceptance causes the vertigo to disappear. His dizziness and inability to act came from his refusal to accept reality and commit himself to it. It is, Hitchcock suggests, the dangerous result of preferring fantasy, whether in life or in the movies.

When audiences leave *Psycho*, the mood of the film remains with them. Suddenly everything becomes threatening, and for a few days taking a shower can become an anxious experience. Our sense of safety has been shaken. Also, we feel vaguely uncomfortable. We wanted horror, we wanted blood, but not that much, and not in that unexpected, irrational way. Our assurance about the world and ourselves has been questioned. Behind the facade of our common, orderly day lies chaos. Beneath our respectable personalities wait impulses and instincts that can destroy us. For Hitchcock it is the basis of a moral vision. Aware of the possibilities, we can guard against them. Even more effectively, we can do so with someone else. At the end of each film two people who have survived the Hitchcock hell come together. It is human relationship, based on self-knowledge, that stands against the instability and dangers of this world.

**Arthur
Penn**

(2028)

Penn's characters are basically good, though inarticulate, people who can't understand the artificial world that imprisons them. Helen Keller (Patty Duke) in The Miracle Worker (1962) can know the world only through touch. Above: the basic struggle on how to free Helen from her "prison" is between her mother (Inga Swenson) and Annie (Anne Bancroft). Andrew Prine plays Helen's brother James. Right: as in all Penn's films, it is direct, physical contact that provides the most meaningful human expression. Only when the water on her hands and its name are made clear to Helen does she understand what Annie can teach her.

☆ 84

In Bonnie and Clyde (1967), *director Penn jars us into recognizing what violence really is. Bonnie (Faye Dunaway) and Clyde (Warren Beatty) are amateur crooks. We laugh at them as they rob a bank (left). But in the getaway, Clyde kills a guard and our laughter turns to shock. Above: the romance of Bonnie and Clyde, like their legend and the film itself, is based on fantasy and wish fulfillment. Over:* Bonnie and Clyde *creates a legend before our very eyes and shows us, in sickening moments of violence, how empty it really was.*

☆ 87

In one of the many tragicomic episodes of *Little Big Man* (1970), the young Jack Crabb, training for his new profession as gunfighter, trades tall tales with the legendary Wild Bill Hickok in the Deadwood saloon. As they talk, Wild Bill whirls and draws on everything that moves, and Crabb is impressed. It is an amusing scene, a gross exaggeration of a Western cliché, and we are sure nothing will come of it, although if something did, neither we nor Crabb would particularly mind. But then Hickok accidentally pulls the trigger and kills somebody. Suddenly the mood is completely changed. Amusement turns to horror. Breaking out in a cold sweat, startled and terrified by the real thing, Crabb blurts out, "Mr. Hickok. That man's really *dead*." Hickok is unmoved. As he says, he didn't even know the gent. Neither did we, as we don't "know" anyone in a film, but we are still appalled. It is not the victim but the fact of violence that we react to. The dramatic change in our feeling is caused by Penn's turning our idle acceptance of possible violence into a grim confrontation with it, and by making us laugh at something that was never funny at all.

Penn uses the same principle to jar us into recognizing what violence is in the first killing in *Bonnie and Clyde* (1967). Up to this point Bonnie, Clyde, and C. W. Moss have been delightful, rather bumbling criminals. We are in the world of comedy where nothing bad really happens. Bonnie and Clyde amateurishly rob a bank while Moss waits in the getaway car. This rather unconvincing gangster, involved in breaking the law, is still sufficiently controlled by that law to parallel park the car while he is waiting. The incongruity is funny. Then he gets stuck in the parking space. Bonnie and Clyde, pursued by bank guards, run out into the street and suddenly the car isn't there. It is exactly the kind of thing we would expect of them, and perhaps of ourselves if we robbed a bank. There is no evil involved, since the people are attractive and their attempted crime not really serious. If they were repulsive criminal types coldly pulling off a job, our attitude might be different. And the foolish, inept, baby-faced Moss is so cute. As he finally gets the car out and they leap in, a bank guard jumps on the running board. Almost as a reflex, but a reflex we have casually known might operate ever since we first saw his gun, Clyde shoots the guard full in the face. Penn doesn't let us escape the full horror of the action. He gives us a close-up of the man's face blasted open in blood. We aren't ready for it. We can argue that we haven't been prepared, but of course we have. Guns, robberies, a man playing at being a gangster, however charmingly, must inevitably result in violence. Penn takes our comfortable, largely unconscious attraction to violence, so familiar that we can be made to laugh when it is potentially present, and abruptly explodes it. In his first film, *The Left Handed Gun* (1957), Billy the Kid shoots a man with a shotgun. The blast knocks him out of one boot, which remains upright in the middle of the street. A little girl, standing with her mother, giggles at the scene. She is immediately slapped. In Penn's films violence in the midst of laughter is always a slap that brings us back to an awareness of what we are doing. In a modern world inured to violence, it is perhaps the only way, he suggests, to make us come to our senses.

Violence in Arthur Penn's films is always the expression of natural urges and impulses that can find no other means of release. Violence is the result of the repression of true feeling, not of malice or conscious cruelty. As Old Lodge Skins, the Cheyenne chief in *Little Big Man*, says of the white man who massacres Indians, they "do not seem to know where the center of the earth is" and consequently their viciousness comes from being forced to live their lives in squares and straight lines. Penn's characters are basically good, though inarticulate, people who can't understand the artificial world that imprisons them. They are further hindered in coping with that world because they experience life physically, through intuition and feeling, rather than through analytic thought. Thus, unaware of their own needs and unable to express them freely in a society that doesn't value spontaneity and honest emotion, they are forced to communicate in the only way left to them—violently.

Helen Keller in *The Miracle Worker* (1962) is the most dramatic example of such a person. Blind, deaf, and dumb she is a prisoner of her own body. She can know the world only through touch, and when that isn't enough, she erupts into violence. Early in the film Helen's parents are arguing about her, and the girl, intuitively aware of the conflict but unable to say anything to stop it, desperately reaches out and slaps her mother across the face. Later, when she is being forced to use a spoon, she throws a tantrum as the only way she can deal with an overwhelming though dimly understood situation. Even Annie Sullivan, the woman who helps Helen Keller develop into a full human being, functions as a result of such frustration. Herself imprisoned as a helpless child in an asylum for the mentally ill, she sees and feels as Helen does, and thus can teach her to communicate. The climax of the film comes when Helen learns from her the connection between finger-spelled words and the objects they represent. As in all Penn's films, it is direct, physical contact that provides the surest, most honest human expression.

William Bonney (Billy the Kid) in *The Left Handed Gun* is as intellectually limited as Helen Keller was physically, and as much an unconscious victim of his own inadequacy. He can't think clearly. Like so many Penn characters—Mickey in *Mickey One* (1964), Anna and Bubber Reeves in *The Chase* (1965), Clyde Barrow in *Bonnie and Clyde,* the hippies in *Alice's Restaurant* (1969), and the Cheyenne in *Little Big Man*—Billy operates naively on instinct and solely in terms of what he sees and feels. He draws no conclusions about people or events, because he doesn't want to exploit them, has no need to manipulate them for his personal ends. Like a child, he is unable to disguise his emotions or subject them to the demands of a practical intelligence. He senses things as an animal would and reacts physically, not theoretically, to the world. He can't read, a sign of his lack of socialization, and when he asks the meaning of a chapter heading, "Through a Glass Darkly," in a book his friend Tunstall is reading, the older man tells him it is "something you can see that you can't make out." It is the central problem for all of Penn's primitive characters. They have only two choices. Either they accept what they can't make out, and are persecuted or killed; or they fight against what they see without being able to make it out, and commit a kind of suicide.

Penn's disenchantment with society begins in *The Left Handed Gun* and grows into a hopeless resignation through the rest of his films. Sheriff Pat Garrett, an established member of the community, is an admirable figure. Although he understands and sympathizes with Billy, he also sees the value of social order and self-restraint. His ambivalent attitude toward Billy—he both admires and disapproves of him—is shared by the audience. The irresolvable conflict between these two valid points of view is shown in the scene of Garrett's wedding, a symbol of the social institutions Billy threatens. Garrett tells him that there will be no shooting at the affair. But when Billy sees one of the men responsible for the murder of his friend Tunstall, he is unable to restrain his impulse for revenge. Billy shoots the man, and Sheriff Garrett eventually turns on him. Billy is wrong, and though society isn't right, he has no place in it. He faces this fact when confronted by his only remaining friend at the end of the film. When Garrett draws, Billy doesn't bother to defend himself. Like Mickey at the conclusion of *Mickey One*, he stands dazed and confused, accepting the judgment of a society he doesn't understand.

Sheriff Calder in *The Chase* is Pat Garrett in an impossible situation. It is almost the same Texas town a hundred years later. Money and moral respectability have taken over, and the people are imprisoned in their social roles. They have become victims of their own empty values, and are suffering from emotional asphyxiation. Signs of tension and frustration are everywhere. In an early scene in Val Rogers's impressively appointed bank, business being conducted politely and with proper decorum, the powerful forces that lie just below the surface begin to emerge. Emily Stewart, wife of one vice-president and mistress of another, berates her husband for his cowardice and makes a date with her lover in a voice almost audible enough for everyone to hear. We have the sense that she wants them to hear it though she doesn't quite dare, wants to rip away all social pretense so that she can breathe. We are made to share her frustration, hoping she will shout it out and afraid that she will.

At the three parties—which are presented in telling counterpoint to highlight their similarity—the tensions that will lead to violence mount to the breaking point. Val Rogers's stiff, formal dinner party, the guests rigidly repressed, is as claustrophobic and coercive as the oil empire he dominates. His son, forced into a disastrous marriage, his life run by a blindly authoritarian father, finally flees to be with one of the few natural figures in the film, Anna Reeves. The Stewarts' party, a barely disguised orgy of lust and death, is a dark reflection of Rogers's. By passively accepting his false values, they live in a sexual and moral hell that can only explode into destruction and murder. The teen-age party next door is a pale copy of theirs, and when the gun goes off as their parents play at killing Bubber Reeves, they flood in excitedly, completing the circle. They will all be accomplices in the violence that follows, and in destroying the best among them, they will destroy themselves.

Bubber Reeves, and by extension Calder, is the natural object of their hatred. He is the only one with any spontaneity left and the only one who acts on it. Like Billy the Kid, he is both secretly admired and socially condemned. Calder stands between the town and its scapegoat-hero. Like Garrett, he represents law and order, but he no longer has community sanction for these values. His brutal beating by the townspeople shocks us as much by its meaning as by its savagery. When, later in the film, he beats the man who killed Bubber Reeves, we realize that he has been defeated. His own self-control was the only thing that kept him from being corrupted by the people around him. There is nothing more he can do. He must leave in disgust and despair. As his wife leads him away saying with quiet resignation, "Calder, let's go. Come on," Penn turns his back on any hope for a sane society.

In *Bonnie and Clyde* violence is an act of rebellion against a corrupt and sterile society. In his two subsequent films he offers escape as the only remaining alternative. The hippies in *Alice's Restaurant* attempt to live peacefully on the fringes of society. It is a temporary solution at best. Having failed in Stockbridge, Alice is moving on to Vermont. Arlo, sensing the futility of escape, turns, as Calder and Jake Rogers and Clyde Barrow did before him, to a woman for relief. Jack Crabb in *Little Big Man* has managed to survive the corruption of America through continual deception. Having no identity, he has assumed whatever guise, Indian or Indian fighter, that will keep him alive. He has become, in old age, an artifact that can only tell stories. He makes the truth bearable by turning fact into legend and his tales, like Penn's films, full of humor and violence, help him to keep a precarious sanity. The humor makes us aware of the ugliness of the violence, and the violence makes the humor necessary. The legend allows us to escape from reality and also forces us to confront that reality in a new way. It is the underlying principle of Arthur Penn's art.

Like John Ford and Orson Welles, Penn deals with the creation of myth. He has said that "the idea of what happened behind the legends has always interested me." The legendary figures in his films are those people who play out the frustrated desires of society. It is a highly contradictory situation. The outlaw, who disregards social rules and lives freely according to his own emotional needs—Billy the Kid, Bubber Reeves, Bonnie and Clyde—becomes both a hero and a threat to society. He is a hero because he lives as we would like to, indulging those impulses that we cannot. He is a threat because in glorifying him, we become aware of our frustration and realize we can do nothing about it. The violent criminal symbolizes this contradiction to an even greater extent. Violent crimes can express our own anger and resentment at the social laws that restrict us. We partly approve of such destructive behavior. Yet we also condemn it, because it is personally and socially dangerous, and because we don't like to think that we share such violent instincts. When we do destroy the outlaw, however, we often do it violently, thus releasing the same instincts that we condemn in him, only we justify them by the fact that we are dispensing justice. It is this complicated relationship between society and criminal, and between movie audience and criminal character, that Penn explores in his films.

The real Bonnie Parker was a hard, sadistic, hatchet-faced woman who smoked cigars and had a tattoo on her thigh. Clyde Barrow was a short, weak, grotesquely ugly man who was a homosexual. With C. W. Moss they formed a bizarre, sado-masochistic threesome. These are the facts. Arthur Penn isn't as concerned with the facts as with the legend that was created about them, both in their lifetimes and afterward. What was it about these two killers that appealed to the public of the 1930s and that would appeal to the movie-going public of the 1960s? We identify not with what they were, but what we want them to be—beautiful, vital, loving, and free. Ironically, if they are that way, then their crimes and their eventual bloody death will seem even more horrible and pointless. We do not want the facts but the legend, and in *Bonnie and Clyde* Penn gives us the legend in terms we will never forget.

The opening credits of *Bonnie and Clyde* establish the fragile connection between past and present, reality and myth. In total silence we are shown the innocent family portraits of the Parkers and the Barrows. They resemble our own family albums, and we easily identify with them. These are not queer or abnormal people but just folks like us. Our heroes, for better or worse, will become exact reflections of ourselves. The frozen photographs, distanced from us by their lack of color and their period look, slowly become tinged with red, a suggestion of what is to come. We are led gradually from the past into the present, from the already dead to the fictionally living, from our own reality into that of the film. We are allowed to escape, but into a lovely nightmare.

Clyde's title card dissolves into an extreme close-up of garish red lips, our first and most revealing view of Bonnie. They are coarse and too heavily made up, but there is a sensuality that comes from their very vulgarity. The next shot shows us Bonnie in the mirror admiring herself, her cosmetic image her only real self. The camera pulls back abruptly to show her face and shoulders from a low-angle position, emphasizing the weight of the physical—and by extension social—environment that crushes her. When she turns and throws herself on the bed, we get the sense, from sharp cuts and uncomfortable camera angles, of a caged animal, restless, tense, helplessly trapped in her shabby room. A severe close-up shows her caught behind the bars of her bed, and when she starts beating on them, we feel her fury and frustration. It is appropriate for her, and typical of Penn, that her emotions are expressed in a purely physical way.

Arthur Penn is a physical director. He makes us experience the feelings and condition of his characters through their gestures, the way they stand, move their bodies, walk, touch each other. The way Clyde leans against a wooden post when Bonnie first approaches him, his shoulders hunched protectively, his face closed and suspicious behind the jauntily uptilted toothpick, his hands draped tensely but casually over the gun. The way Bonnie stands before him, her body tentative but eager, her hands held out in a combination of authority and hesitance toward the forbidden weapon. Even their first exchange of glances through the window, without a word being spoken, has a physical impact—a direct, palpable connection has been made.

The scene continues to establish the film's basic themes in the most economical, purely visual way. From within the dark, constricting room Clyde is seen in long shot standing by the car—symbol of speed and release—surrounded by air and space and sunshine on a beautiful spring day. He represents her only hope for escape. When Bonnie stands provocatively naked behind the curtain and calls down a challenge to him, he responds with unconvincing arrogance, and their future relationship is defined. She rushes down the twisting stairway and flings herself into the sunlight, pausing a moment as she realizes what she is about to do. The decision, as all the important decisions in Penn's films, is made by her body. Its momentum carries her forward, her emotions too strong for her mind to control. When she steps off the porch and into Clyde's world, she sets into motion an adventure that neither she nor we can predict will end in misery and death.

Their first conversation, falsely bright and self-conscious, begins the pretense that will trap them. Clyde pretends to be a confident, experienced ex-convict, Bonnie a shy, proud, dignified lady. Their romance, like their legend and the film itself, is based on fantasy and wish fulfillment. Bonnie, frustrated and helpless, without any resources of her own except a pretty face and a willingness to try anything, identifies with someone she— and we—thinks is powerful and free. Clyde, a petty crook, sexually impotent and deeply unsure of himself, sees her as a beautiful consort and admirer, the woman who can convince him that he is actually what he pretends to be.

Through the rest of the film they try, with our approval and complicity, to turn themselves into legends, posing for pictures, reading their press clippings, robbing banks as they think real criminals do. It is touching and charming until the legend begins to overwhelm them and takes on a life of its own. Then they become victims of their own actions. Bonnie can't go home. Clyde is in fact a hunted killer. Buck is shot down and Blanche arrested. When Clyde tells the farmer, "We rob banks," he is frankly awed at what he has become. Yet it is what he, and we, wanted all along. It is significant that he becomes sexually potent after Bonnie writes the poem immortalizing them. She has made the myth real for him, and the world—public, newspapers, the movie audience—has conspired to help her. Like children, they have been playing at being outlaws. But when they kill and are killed, we are forced to see the ugliness that underlies the fairy tale. Penn makes clear "what happened behind the legends." The film creates a legend before our very eyes and shows us, in those sickening moments of violence, how empty it really was.

The final scene is conceived as an excruciating ballet of death. The slow-motion photography and extremely realistic detail make it both fascinating and horrible. Fascinating as myth, horrible as life. It is the same double view of them we have from the first shooting, and sums up the ambivalent attitude that we hold toward killers who have passed into legend. To make us see that violence can be both beautiful and ugly, both attractive and repulsive, is to make us wary of its deceptive power.

Arthur Penn leaves them, finally, frozen in time, as befits a legend. He wants us to remember them that way. To destroy the myth would allow us to discount it and be free to believe in others. To let it linger, false and seductive, is to make us examine our need for such things. What audiences remember years later are not the gay times of Bonnie and Clyde, but their bodies tossed like torn dolls by despoiling machine gun fire. Penn is perhaps the cinema's most mature and complex student of violence. He shows it, he analyzes it, and he proves that it isn't much fun.

Stanley Kubrick

Kubrick's characters, like those in an allegory, generally fall into three classes of captivity. One class is the soldiers in Paths of Glory (1957), used by their superiors in war. George Macready (left) plays the ambitious General Mireau who sacrifices his men for his own glory. Caught helplessly in the middle are the passionate, dedicated men who pursue their goal whatever the cost. Above, Kirk Douglas (right) plays the honest Colonel Dax.

☆ 101

Left: playing with the lives of Mireau and Dax is the corrupt, vain man of power General Broulard (Adolphe Menjou). Major Saint-Auban (Richard Anderson, wearing riding boots) is another pawn. Most characters in Kubrick's films are remembered by distinctive details—Dax futilely blowing his whistle as he runs across the deadly no-man's-land (above).

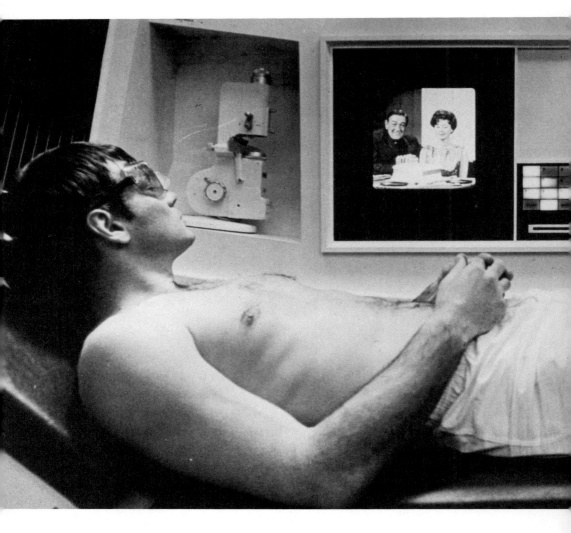

Dr. Heywood Floyd (William Sylvester), right, with other scientists gazes at the monolith that represents a cosmic intelligence in 2001: A Space Odyssey *(1968). Astronaut Frank Poole (Gary Lockwood), above, relaxes and gets sun-lamp treatment aboard the space craft* Discovery, *while his parents televise their birthday greetings to him—an illustration of how mechanistic society destroys emotional existence.*

Stanley Kubrick sees films as closer to music than other art forms. 2001: A Space Odyssey *demonstrates how form and cinematic elements provide the "meaning" of a movie. Keir Dullea plays David Bowman, the surviving astronaut.*

Some film-makers think that the motion picture is closer to the novel than to the other art forms because of its use of plot, characters, and its freedom of movement through time and space. Others consider it closest to theater, since it uses actors and dialogue and emphasizes the conflict between people seen physically, from the outside. Still others see it as resembling painting, creating meaningful pictures within a set frame. Stanley Kubrick sees films as closest to music. He has said that "a film is—or should be—more like music than like fiction. It should be a progression of moods and feelings. The theme, what's behind the emotion, the meaning, all that comes later. After you've walked out of the theater, maybe the next day or a week later, maybe without ever realizing it, you somehow get what the film-maker has been trying to tell you" (Peter Lyon, "The Astonishing Stanley Kubrick," *Holiday*, February 1964).

Like music, his films are highly stylized and depend for their effect primarily on structure, the way the parts are put together. For Kubrick the form and the cinematic elements *are* the meaning of the film, rather than the story or the psychology or what the people say before the cameras. As he explained about the making of *2001: A Space Odyssey* (1968), a film that contains almost no dialogue and the barest narrative thread: "I tried to create a *visual experience,* one that bypasses verbalized pigeon-holing and directly penetrates the subconscious with an emotional and philosophic content. . . . I intended the film to be an intensely subjective experience that reaches the viewer at an inner level of consciousness, just as music does" (*Playboy* interview, quoted in Jerome Agel, *The Making of Kubrick's 2001* [New York: New American Library, 1972]). Thus each of the filmic elements—lighting, camerawork, settings, editing—like the notes and movements in a musical composition make up the "meaning" of the film.

Kubrick is particularly well-trained to take this approach. At sixteen he became a photographer-journalist for *Look* magazine, which gave him a solid foundation in the use of the camera and in developing an eye for illustrative detail. He studied lighting and held a union card as a lighting cameraman. He has read deeply in the works of Pudovkin and Eisenstein to learn film editing. He studied all the material he could find on directing actors, particularly books on the great Russian theater director, Stanislavski. He has seen just about every movie made in every language. He was forced, in the first three films he made, to do everything himself because of lack of funds. He remembers of his first nondocumentary film, made in 1953, that "the entire crew of *Fear and Desire* consisted of myself as director, lighting cameraman, operator, administrator, make-up man, wardrobe, hairdresser, prop man, unit chauffeur, et cetera" (Alexander Walker, *Stanley Kubrick Directs* [New York: Harcourt Brace Jovanovich, 1971]). The experience was invaluable, and he has insisted on total control of every film made since, either doing every task himself or closely supervising others. Equally important, Kubrick is a master chess player. He conceives and designs his films almost as a chess game, each move carefully thought out, the entire plan—again, like a musical composition—designed beforehand, and each decision contributing to the overall strategy.

The basic element in Kubrick's films is structure, both the way one shot is juxtaposed against another in a scene, and the way the scenes are related to each other. He builds this structure by editing, the process he considers the most important and distinctive thing about films. He has said: "I love editing, I think I like it more than any other phase of film-making. If I wanted to be frivolous, I might say that everything that precedes editing is merely a way of producing film to edit. Editing is the only unique aspect of film-making which does not resemble any other form—a point so important it cannot be over-stressed. . . . It can make or break a film" (Walker, *Stanley Kubrick Directs*).

The tension and suspense of his third movie, *The Killing* (1956), a crime thriller, depends on such editing. Five men have decided to rob a racetrack. Kubrick begins the film with a shot of the horses leaving the stables and moving into position at the starting gate, a scene he will repeatedly insert throughout the movie, like a musical motif, to indicate new stages in the action. He introduces the gang members in five quickly succeeding scenes, choosing the details that most economically express their characters. The actual robbery is presented in three different overlapping scenes; each starts at the same instant and continues to completion before switching to the next scene, in which another man is doing his job at the same time. It is the same method he will use in *Dr. Strangelove* (1964), eight years later, cutting back and forth from the War Room to the B-52 bomber to Ripper's office at Burpleston Air Force Base, and during the battle in *Paths of Glory* (1957), switching from the generals in the chateau to the trenches at the front lines to the battlefield itself. Kubrick is working against time in presenting these scenes, as the characters in the films are themselves working against time to complete their tasks.

His structural editing can also be seen in the way he splices shots together to make a point. In *2001* the two astronauts go into a soundproof pod in their spaceship to confer in private about the computer, HAL-9000, which is dangerously malfunctioning. Through the glass we see them facing each other—in the same crouched position as the frightened apes earlier in the film —discussing what to do. We can't hear them and we assume neither can the computer. But then Kubrick cuts to a close-up of their mouths and back to a close-up of the machine's glowing eye. We realize that it is reading their lips. The fact, terrifying in itself, is made even more ominous by the abrupt, silent way it is conveyed in purely visual terms.

In a scene in *A Clockwork Orange* (1971) that closely resembles the one in which HAL watches the astronauts, we see Alex, thinking he is safe and unobserved in the bathtub, break out into "Singing in the Rain." Kubrick cuts to the author downstairs, who suddenly recognizes the voice and the tune as the same he heard when his wife was raped, and we know that he will try to kill his unsuspecting guest. More than in any of the other films, this device is used in *Dr. Strangelove*, to heighten the drama and humor within the individual scenes and let them comment on each other. Taken singly they are ridiculous enough, but in association they become totally absurd.

As a photo-journalist Kubrick had to be able to select those gestures and physical details that could most efficiently tell his story. He uses this visual shorthand in all his films. As early as his second movie, *Killer's Kiss* (1955), he indicates the personality and relationship of the two main characters through a number of short, wordless scenes. At the beginning Davy Gordon, a failing prizefighter, is in his drab rented room preparing for the night's fight. He reads the paper without interest and then shaves listlessly—we see photos of his home, father, and girl friend stuck in the mirror, an instant biography and comment on his situation—and as he dresses, glances out the window. A dance-hall girl lives across the court, and through the window he can see her preparing for her evening's work. She also watches him. Later, after losing the fight, he returns to his room and lies on the bed in the dark. He is lonely, defeated, hopeless. Again he watches the girl in her brightly lit apartment as she moves about, listening to cheerful music, finally undressing for bed. To him the scene is a vision of warmth, security, and happiness. From her gestures and forced energy, and the fact that she lets herself be watched, we know that she is equally desperate, alone, and unhappy. Yet to Davy she seems unattainable, everything he wants but cannot have.

Kubrick uses the same kind of selective imagery for the same purpose in *Lolita* (1962), when Humbert Humbert surreptitiously watches the young girl he loves; in *Paths of Glory* when Dax stands outside the theater watching his men enjoy an innocent world he cannot share; and most directly in *A Clockwork Orange* when Alex, undergoing the Ludovico Treatment is forced to watch scenes of sex and violence that once excited him but now make him sick.

Most characters in Kubrick films are remembered by distinctive details—George C. Scott thumping his bare stomach when he answers the phone at the beginning of *Dr. Strangelove,* Dr. Strangelove's unmanageable mechanical arm jerking up to strangle him, the boredom with which Bowman jogs, reads, eats, does his tasks in a spaceship bound for Jupiter in *2001,* Dax futilely blowing his whistle as he runs across the deadly no-man's-land in *Paths of Glory.* No narration or dialogue is needed. The carefully selected image is enough.

As a tournament chess player Kubrick has a highly developed sense of time and space. In chess, as in films, the moves must be made during a certain time. Davy must save Gloria before she's killed in *Killer's Kiss,* the robbery is a split-second job in *The Killing,* Dax must save the convicted men before they are executed in *Paths of Glory,* Humbert is constantly frustrated by the loss of time in *Lolita,* the plane must be called back before it bombs Russia in *Dr. Strangelove,* time is endless and finally transcended in *2001,* time is a vacuum to be filled with violence in *A Clockwork Orange.* And the movement of the pieces is restricted to the limits of the board and the space available within its confines.

Utilization of space both on the screen and in the film is equally important in these movies. The wide screen of *2001,* Super Panavision in Cinerama, is used as a window through which the audience looks into the limitless space of the universe. The stunning effect of the light streaming toward us in Bowman's trip to Jupiter is made possible by the confinement of the screen—we have the sense that the cosmic landscape is flooding past us and disappearing behind us into a limitless void. Kubrick first used this visual technique in Davy's dream in *Killer's Kiss* as the nightmarish streets, filmed in negative, rush past us as he races forward. In *Dr. Strangelove* the flight of the low-flying plane, with the polar wastes racing by below us, gives the same feeling of hurtling forward out of control. The actual space on the screen contributes to this feeling. Were we really in the plane, with vision to the sides, the effect would be far less startling.

In *Dr. Strangelove* there are three defining spaces. In the enormous War Room, the most powerful men in America are helpless; they have the space but can't use it. They are mocked by it. The men crushed into the B-52 have no space at all, although outside is all the space they could ever need. They are also restricted by their blind devotion to duty, as much as by the narrow fuselage. General Ripper's office, like his paranoid mind, is closed and literally being attacked from outside. He retreats into an even smaller space, the bathroom, to shoot himself. Given his imprisoning madness and its consequences, he has nowhere else to go.

This theme of physical and symbolic entrapment occurs in most of Kubrick's films. In the two early crime-movies the protagonists are trapped within the hostile confines of an oppressive city and of their own limited lives. In *Lolita* Humbert and Lolita are trapped in their car as in their relationship, although both should be liberating. Most dramatically, the astronauts of *2001*, surrounded by an infinity of space, are cramped within their space suits, their tiny space pods, and the spaceship no larger than a small house. This oppressive confinement is the moral theme of Kubrick's films. Man is a prisoner of his obsessive passions and rigid thinking, and from them derive his bureaucracies, his technology, and his too narrow definition of himself. He must be helped, as by the monolith in *2001*, to break out of this self-imposed imprisonment in order to develop and be free.

Kubrick's characters, like those in an allegory, fall generally into three classes of captivity. There are the passive victims who, through ignorance or blind obedience, allow themselves to be exploited and sacrificed by others: the soldiers in *Paths of Glory*, used by their superiors whether in war or peace;

Dolores Haze in *Lolita,* the pawn in an erotic game between her mother, Humbert, and Quilty; the B-52 crewmen in *Dr. Strangelove,* who have been trained to kill themselves zealously; the scientists and frozen astronauts in *2001,* who have lost all identity by submitting minds and bodies to a higher authority; and the citizens, both criminal and law-abiding, in the futuristic society of *A Clockwork Orange.*

Contemptuously playing with their lives are the corrupt, vain, cynical men of power—Quilty (*Lolita*), General Broulard and General Mireau (*Paths of Glory*), Dr. Strangelove and General Turgidson (*Dr. Strangelove*), the computer HAL-9000 and his designers on earth (*2001*), and the Interior Minister and his government (*A Clockwork Orange*). Caught helplessly in the middle are the passionate, direct, dedicated men who pursue their goal whatever the cost. They are always sadly defeated. Colonel Dax in *Paths of Glory,* although he briefly rebels against the higher command, continues to work their will by leading his men back into war to be killed. In *Dr. Strangelove* Major Kong, a simplified extension of Dax, is so enthusiastically if naively committed to his job that he blows up the world. Humbert, driven by his desire for Lolita, remains a compassionate, faithful lover through everything, and ends broken and alone. Alex, repulsive as his behavior may be, is the one genuinely passionate figure in the mechanical society of *A Clockwork Orange,* and finally even he is made to conform, not by the Ludovico method, but by his own free will. Only Major David Bowman in *2001,* the perfectly programmed human being, is able, through the mysterious intervention of a supernatural power, to break through the boundaries of time, space, and human personality.

The irony that underlies and shapes Kubrick's films is that all these characters are equally victims of an absurd, insane world. They are creatures in a fairy tale that makes no sense. Life is an Alice in Wonderland chess game that seems logical only to those who, like Broulard and Strangelove and Quilty, play without questioning it. In *Paths of Glory* Mireau arrogantly sacrifices his men and is then himself sacrificed. Roget, who should be shot, is the head of a firing squad. Dax, whose whole life is based on morality, resorts to blackmail to win his case. The terms are those of a chess game. Mireau's inhuman mathematics that 25 percent of his men will be killed leaving the trenches, 25 percent crossing the fields, and another 25 percent taking the Ant Hill, leaving enough to occupy it, are echoed in General Turgidson's impersonal calculation in *Dr. Strangelove*: "I am not saying we wouldn't get our hair mussed. I am saying only ten to twenty million people killed, tops, depending on the breaks."

There is no logic anywhere. When his soldiers retreat under murderous fire, Mireau orders his own gunners to bombard them from the rear. "If those little sweethearts won't face German bullets," he snarls, "they'll face French ones." After the debacle he accuses what few men remain of cowardice, and decides to shoot ten from each company as an object lesson. He is bargained down, as if he were selling eggs, to accepting only three men from the whole battalion. When Dax, a lawyer in civilian life, tries to defend them before the court-martial, he realizes how bizarre and inflexible the rules of the game are. The final irony, after the men are executed and Dax exposes Mireau's order to turn his artillery on his own army, is that Broulard offers him Mireau's job, thinking that was what he was after all along. In this kind of world Dax, however honest and humane, is crazy in terms of the values accepted by everyone else. He returns to combat, checkmated because he didn't know it was only a game.

Innumerable scenes in Kubrick's films give a visual statement of this insanity. In his first film, *Fear and Desire*, war is seen as a strangely confused dream, Corby and Fletcher killing an enemy general and his aide who turn out to be themselves. The final scene, in which the raft drifts out of the fog, carrying the dead Mac and the insane Sidney, is filmed as a moment glimpsed in Dante's hell. In *Killer's Kiss* Davy and Vince fight it out in a mannequin factory, using dismembered arms and legs as weapons in the midst of a surrealistic setting of frozen dummies. The battle for no-man's-land in *Paths of Glory* is one of the most horrifying and nightmarish scenes of war ever filmed. The men run, dodge, crawl, topple, fall grotesquely in a pitted, ruined landscape that reduces everything—old and new corpses, twisted wire, blasted fortifications, torn bits of clothing and fragments of equipment, wounded and dying men—to the same terrible level of madness. In the middle of it Dax, the one sane but foolish man, remains upright and urges his men on.

This surrealistic view of the world becomes clearer in the later films. The murder scene that begins *Lolita* takes place in Quilty's weirdly furnished house. His death turns into a burlesque as he plays Ping-Pong, imitates Gaby Hayes, pulls on boxing gloves, demoniacally plays Chopin on the piano, crawls up the stairs and finally dies behind a bullet-riddled painting of a young girl. Like HAL-9000 in its last pathetic moments and President Muffley in his War Room, he employs every possible device to stave off death. Perhaps the two most surrealistic moments in American cinema are in the scene in 2001 in which a man kills a computer that is begging for its life while it regresses into childhood, and in the unforgettable scene in *Dr. Strangelove* in which Major King Kong, a hydrogen bomb between his legs and a ten-gallon hat in his hand, plummets to earth whooping out a war cry. Kubrick tries, through extreme stylization of form and exaggeration and juxtaposition of images, to show us how bizarre this world is.

The ironic vision that emerged as tragedy in *Paths of Glory* and tragicomedy in *Lolita* turns to grim comedy in *Dr. Strangelove*. In this film Kubrick shows attitudes and actions that might seem normal to us in ordinary situations. By placing them in an absurd but logical context, given the wild logic we live by, he reveals how insane they really are. To do this, Kubrick uses two major techniques of satire. He takes familiar things and renders them grotesque against the possibility of nuclear holocaust, and he takes attitudes to their extreme to show how they are responsible for our madness in the first place. In the middle of a conference about the fate of the world, General Turgidson's phone rings. It is his impatient mistress. As concerned with placating her as with saving humanity he whispers into the phone, "Look baby, I can't talk to you now—my President needs me. Of course it isn't purely physical, I deeply respect you as a human being. Don't forget to say your prayers." With a billion lives hanging in the balance, Bat Guano won't let Captain Mandrake break into a Coke machine to get a dime to call the President with the recall code. Private property is sacred. Major Kong promises his crew a promotion if they successfully complete the mission that will destroy them. President Muffley calls the Russian Premier with the dreadful news and gets bogged down in soothing his feelings: "Why do you think I'm calling you—just to say hello? Of course I like to speak to you, of course I like to say hello. I'm just calling up to tell you something terrible has happened. It's a friendly call, of course it's a friendly call. Listen, if it wasn't friendly you probably wouldn't have even got it."

By changing the context of the thoroughly familiar, Kubrick shows how unexpectedly strange it can be. More importantly, through logical extension he exposes the reasons for our predicament. General Ripper's sexual insecurity leads to a paranoid theory of "precious bodily fluids" which are being poisoned through water fluoridation by Communist agents, and of his "essence" which is being stolen by women. The consequence of such masculinity fears is the aggressive posture of his nation, which leads to world war. The other characters share his obsession. Bat Guano almost prevents Mandrake from sending the message that will stop the plane, because he thinks the Englishman is a "prevert." Turgidson sees nuclear power as an extension of his own sexual potency. Dr. Strangelove, physically and morally crippled, becomes excited only at the possibility of living in a mine shaft with ten women to every man. The two planes symbolically copulating in the opening shot, and the phallic bomb gripped between Major Kong's legs at the end, result in the cosmic orgasm of the bomb blast, which miraculously lets Strangelove walk again. Repression of emotion and the cynical manipulation of human beings have produced mechanical men living in a deadly mechanical society. It is the theme that will be treated more fully in Kubrick's next two films.

In *2001: A Space Odyssey* humanity has become so completely mechanized that computers are more human than people. There are still some comic elements—the scientists posing for a conventional tourist picture against the moon monolith, Major Poole burning his surprisingly still sensitive flesh on a totally computerized meal—but this is not a satire. Society has gone too far for that. Our civilization has come to an end, turned flat and weary and stale. There is no energy, no purpose, no creative intelligence. Each individual is merely a bored, faceless cog in a technological system. Kubrick conceived this film as a "mythological documentary," a modern legend of the origin and future of humankind. It is both realistic as a photo-essay and imaginary as a fable. It is essentially a religious movie. Replacing the traditional God of world religions is a cosmic intelligence that influences human evolution at certain pivotal moments. When the ape has evolved as far as it can as an instinctual animal, the first monolith appears, giving the power of creative intelligence that produces the tool-weapon. When that tool has been sophisticated as far as the human mind can conceive—the dramatic cut from the bone thrown into the air to the spaceship resembling it symbolizes this development—the monolith appears again to force humanity on to the next stage. Major Bowman, lacking character and personality as he is, still retains enough feeling to try to rescue his colleague, enough ingenuity to reenter the spaceship after he has been locked out, and enough dedication and courage to continue on his journey, to be chosen as the new human being. On the trip to Jupiter he transcends space, and once arrived there, he transcends time, watching himself age in minutes. As he dies, the monolith appears, he reaches out to it in greeting and gratitude, and is reborn into a creature that transcends his previous humanity. The change from human to Star Child is as drastic as from ape to human: the Star Child will continue our evolution with a radically new intelligence.

The theme of mechanistic society destroying emotional existence is explored in a less futuristic period in *A Clockwork Orange*. In *2001* Kubrick gives us HAL-9000, a machine that functions as a human; in the later film he presents people who function as machines. As the writer in the film explains, human beings have become clockwork oranges, natural beings turned by a repressive society and an all-powerful technology into machines. Both the political left and right are predictable and equally destructive. Life has become utopian but dull; relaxation is dispensed in drug-milk bars and comfort enjoyed in featureless apartments. Art has no connection with life and thus no meaning: the cold plastic female figures in the Korova Milkbar serve as tables, the cat lady won't let Alex touch her absurd white plastic sculpture of a ticking penis, the author writes his novel on an IBM typewriter.

Alex is the extreme product of such a society. With no possible outlets for his innate passion and instincts, he turns to ultraviolence. But such behavior—as in *Dr. Strangelove*——threatens the existence of the very society that it reflects and that produced it. Thus Alex must be scientifically programmed to abhor sex and violence, even if it means he no longer has the capacity to enjoy art or the ability to defend himself. He must be turned into a safe, inoffensive clockwork orange. Before his chemical conversion he has free will. But free will is dangerous. The Ludovico Treatment replaces it. Afterward he is no longer dangerous, but he is no longer a human being.

As a result of his attempted suicide, he returns to his previous state. Another sanction must be found to make him conform to his society. He is co-opted into the establishment by the Interior Minister, who promises him a high-paying job if he cooperates. Finally, seeing the power of a society that offers only the alternatives of prison, drug mindlessness, and hypocritical conformity, he saves what he can. He agrees. At least this will allow him to have sex and listen to Beethoven. His last line, and the end of the movie, is his gleeful statement, "I was cured after all." Cured of any illusion about his society or the possibility of any sanity in it. Kubrick's films show that insanity so graphically that perhaps by exposing it they can help to end it.

The New
Directors

In The Last Picture Show *(1971), Bogdanovich presents a nos-talgic re-creation of a Texas town in the 1950s. Left: Timothy Bottoms plays the innocent teen-ager befriended by the lonely Cloris Leachman. Above: Bogdanovich shows life in a small Texas town as boring and mediocre. To help pass the time, two high school seniors, Jeff Bridges (left) and Timothy Bottoms (right), take advantage of the mute Sam Bottoms (center).*

☆ 123

In The Godfather (1972), Francis Ford Coppola wanted to show how a basically good man, Don Corleone (Marlon Brando), could be corrupted by the violent world around him. At the left is James Caan. The Godfather had something serious to say; it showed the true character of organized violence. Al Pacino (above right) played Michael Corleone, who followed in his father's footsteps.

3a

The most innovative, truly original film-maker today is possibly
Robert Altman. In McCabe and Mrs. Miller (1971), Warren
Beatty takes the part of John McCabe, the owner of a small-
town bordello. These are some of his prostitutes. Altman in
California Split (1974) captures the raw taste and feel of Las
Vegas. George Segal and Elliot Gould (with bandaged nose) play
gamblers with empty lives.

☆ 126

The major difference between the newer directors and the men we have discussed so far is that, with a very few exceptions, the younger people have not developed a consistent philosophy or distinctly personal style. Each film they do is a separate project, and whatever ideas and methods they use are dictated by the particular script and story. It is hard to see how Sidney Lumet's *The Defiant Ones, Serpico,* and *Murder on the Orient Express* were made by the same director, fine as these films may be. Besides a slickness of execution, Mike Nichols's *Who's Afraid of Virginia Woolf?, The Graduate, Catch-22,* and *The Day of the Dolphin* have little in common. William Friedkin, Norman Jewison, John Frankenheimer, Sidney J. Furie, and George Roy Hill, to name a few, have not produced identifiable bodies of work. Also, the younger directors have obviously been influenced by the film-makers who came before them. At worst, they merely copy styles, and at best, they incorporate others' techniques to create a new form. In some cases they fail to produce original work because they are so in awe of the classic directors that they can only borrow from them. Finally, many young directors have seen so many movies that the films they make are really about other movies.

A good example of this is Peter Bogdanovich. For years a movie critic and film scholar, he admits that his films are derivative. He has frequently mentioned those directors he learned from—Ford, Welles, Hawks, Hitchcock, Leo McCarey, Fritz Lang, Raoul Walsh—and his films are tributes to them. His first film, *Targets,* is patterned after a Hitchcock thriller; *The Last Picture Show* is in part an attempt to make a Ford Western of the 1940s and in part a throwback to Welles's *The Magnificent Ambersons. What's Up, Doc?* is a screwball comedy of mistaken identity resembling Hawks's films of the 1930s; Bogdanovich refuses to repeat himself, and thus makes films on a variety of subjects and in a variety of styles. The difficulty is that, whereas the earlier directors made films with spontaneous invention, Bogdanovich is self-conscious, and his movies are too neat and carefully manipulated. There is a calculated distance from his characters, a coolness and detachment. His films are entertaining, but you have a sense that he doesn't himself believe in them. They are too well made.

The way in which many of these new directors got their start often explains the kind of films they subsequently made. After doing film reviews, Bogdanovich worked with the king of trash horror movies, Roger Corman, in the 1960s. On the strength of his contribution to Corman's *The Wild Angels*—he rewrote the script, scouted locations, and shot fifteen minutes of the film—Corman agreed to let him make a film of his own. The offer was accompanied by seemingly insuperable conditions. Since the actor Boris Karloff owed Corman two days work for which he had been paid $15,000, Bogdanovich had to use him for twenty minutes of the film. Further, he had to insert another twenty minutes of an unreleased Karloff chiller, *The Terror*. He could do what he liked with the remaining forty minutes on an exceptionally low budget. Showing great ingenuity, Bogdanovich managed to make an interesting film. *Targets* is the story of a deranged assassin who goes berserk with a rifle at a drive-in movie. Of course the movie playing behind the action is *The Terror*, and Karloff is present in a guest appearance. *Targets* is an insightful study of a psychopathic killer, and it established Bogdanovich as a promising young director.

The rest of his films have proved his technical ability but so far show that he lacks the originality and conviction of his mentors. *The Last Picture Show*, a nostalgic re-creation of a Texas town in the 1950s, repeats the theme of Welles's *The Magnificent Ambersons*, the passing of a traditional way of life. For Welles the end of a gracious, civilized period is marked by the coming of the automobile, which symbolizes greed and ugliness. For Bogdanovich the passing of a sentimentalized period of boredom and mediocrity is marked by the advent of television. It is significant that what Bogdanovich sees as the greatest loss is the closing of the town movie theater. The fantasy world of films may be for him what cultivated life was for Orson Welles.

Paper Moon is another attempt to recapture a romanticized earlier time; it depicts the free life of a clever con man and his precocious daughter. The disparity between what Bogdanovich meant to depict and what audiences saw is instructive. He has said that the ending is meant to be sad because the father and daughter, reunited, will simply drive off into a life of absolute disaster. He sees their relationship as destructive, a "terrible man and a misused little girl." Most viewers found their relationship to be warm, affectionate, and thoroughly delightful. Bogdanovich may have wanted to portray the father as a vicious man, but he didn't succeed. He wasn't willing to lose the appealing aspects of the character. Certainly the little girl doesn't seem misused; if anything, she manipulates others. This confusion between purpose and realization in Bogdanovich's films suggests that either he isn't fully committed to his declared themes or he can't effectively present them. Other concerns, such as technique and a desire to be entertaining, obscure his professed deeper meaning.

This can also be seen in his two least-successful films, *Daisy Miller* and *At Long Last Love*. *Daisy Miller*, taken from a short story by Henry James about society at the turn of the century, doesn't have the conviction of a true period picture. It seems more a movie about a movie whose subject is the world of the early 1900s. *At Long Last Love*, a musical based on Cole Porter's songs, is neither a remake of a 1930s musical nor a modern musical about the 1930s. It is, unsatisfactorily, a 1970s nonmusical about a 1930s musical. Perhaps for that reason, Bogdanovich chose for his two stars Burt Reynolds and Cybill Shepherd, two people who can't sing or dance. Bogdanovich has explained that he didn't want to make a real musical but rather a movie about some people who perform because they enjoy it, not because they are talented. Many critics have found this to be a strange, if not bizarre, explanation for a film that fails on all counts. The real explanation may lie in the fact that Bogdanovich cannot believe in these film genres the way older directors did, although he continues to use them.

Francis Ford Coppola, a man of prodigious energy and talent, also lacks that individual imprint. His films are stunningly effective productions and have been financial successes but, taken together, there is no unique Coppola style or system of thought. Like Bogdanovich, he got his start with Roger Corman, and probably knows more about every aspect of film production, both the financial and technical sides, than any other young director. Coppola began making eight-millimeter films at the age of twelve and went on to study theater at college. He attended the UCLA film school—he is the only major director to have graduated from film school—and at the age of twenty-four won an Academy Award for writing the screenplay of *Patton*. His rise was meteoric. In two and a half years he wrote ten scripts for Corman and directed three cheap nudie pictures for him. Finally he was allowed to make his own movie, a cheap horror film, *Dementia 13*. As his project for his master's degree at UCLA, Coppola made his first serious film in 1967, *You're a Big Boy Now*. Copying the frenetic style of Richard Lester's *A Hard Day's Night*, Coppola tried to parody the insane pace of modern life, but ended by creating a superficial entertainment that borrows from, rather than comments on, modern popular culture. Although not profound, the film did show that Coppola had the commercial ability to make profitable Hollywood movies.

In the following year, 1968, he made *Finian's Rainbow*, a sentimental, uninspired musical, which failed at the box office. He then formed his own film company to produce serious low-budget films. The result was *The Rain People*, an earnest if flawed effort. Loading his film crew and cast into trucks, he traveled twenty thousand miles in eighteen weeks, shooting, processing, and editing the film on the road. *The Rain People* concerns a pregnant wife who leaves her husband to find herself, and who in the course of her travels finds instead a series of unsatisfactory men. The movie fails in many departments. Coppola admits that he didn't know how to end it, and the style is pretentious and self-consciously arty. It is filled with film clichés—dramatic cuts that make their point too obviously —and dialogue that is heavily significant. Because the film was both a critical and financial failure, Coppola dissolved his company and returned to Hollywood. But at least he had proved that he could produce an entire film completely on his own.

Coppola's next project, *The Godfather*, established his reputation. It was his purpose to make a popular film that also had something serious to say. He wanted to show the true character of organized violence—its essential lack of excitement and passion—as well as to portray the Mafia realistically. He also wanted to show how two basically good, innocent men, Don Corleone and his son Michael, could be corrupted by the violent worlds they lived in. As anyone who has seen it can attest, it is an extremely effective film. Coppola does not develop mood and character slowly, as he did in *The Rain People*, but uses action and sharp exchanges of dialogue to establish his themes. *The Godfather* also illustrates his theory of a movie made for an active rather than a passive audience. He creates a film in which the viewer can participate, unlike *The Exorcist*, for example, which encourages the audience merely to sit back and be acted upon. There are few angle shots to stimulate audience response. The camera is usually head-on to the scene, with either a three-quarter view of the actor, a full head-to-toe shot, or a simple close-up. Also, Coppola moves his camera as little as possible. A case in point is the scene in which Sonny Corleone is murdered at the toll both. The entire scene is filmed at a distance with a stable camera. The audience participates in the total scene rather than having its attention forced on certain details and its emotions excited by a wildly zooming and panning camera. The death of Don Corleone in the garden is filmed in the same way. The audience is given the scene from a neutral distance, without emphasis, and it can choose whatever it wants to look at. Coppola refuses to manipulate his viewers, he does not try to force them to respond in a preconceived way.

After the enormous commercial success of *The Godfather*, Coppola was able to make a more personal film for himself. The challenge in *The Conversation* was to take an uneventful plot and a noncommunicative character and create an absorbing film almost entirely through the use of the camera. The impersonal, strictly controlled technique reflects the cold, unemotional world of the wiretapper Harry Caul without excessive verbal comment. It is, cinematographically, perhaps Coppola's most interesting film. The project that followed, *The Godfather II*, was at first assumed to mark Coppola's return to profitable movie-making and to be a quick exploitation of the first movie. In fact, as Coppola has suggested, it is a far better film and can stand artistically on its own. Returning to a device he used in *The Rain People*, Coppola alternates actions taking place in two different locations and times. The telling counterpoint of the two related plots, the early years of Don Corleone and the seizure of power by Michael, forms the structure of the drama. Coppola also expands his earlier experiments with light. *The Godfather II* is a dark, foreboding film, and in many scenes part of the shot—for example, a character's face or body—remains obscured in shadow. Coppola believes that you don't have to see every detail in every frame, that there is a "persistance of vision" that allows the audience to fill in what is hidden as they watch it. Again, it is a way of allowing the viewer to participate actively in the movie. At the moment, Francis Ford Coppola is probably the most technically accomplished commercial director in the business.

The most innovative, truly original film-maker today is possibly Robert Altman. He brings a genuinely new approach to the cinema. He has said, "I look at a film as closer to a painting or a piece of music, it's an impression." The experience of viewing an Altman film is different. You don't "follow" it as much as open yourself to it. It leaves you somewhat dazed and confused, you figure it out afterward. The feeling and tone and texture are as important to Altman as character and plot. As he explains, "The audience will . . . simply let the film wash over them." Altman tries, like Martin Scorsese and John Cassavetes, to make "real" movies, films that seem to be recording what is happening as it happens. In viewing Scorsese's *Mean Streets* or Altman's *MASH*, you don't have a sense that you are watching a structured movie but that you are actually seeing the events take place. This is extraordinarily difficult to do. Home movies that we might take of the family usually look unreal when we show them. Somehow the naturalness and spontaneity have been lost. The camera has a perverse way of transforming real life into something that looks false and artificial. In order to recapture that freshness and immediacy, the film-maker must use the camera to translate the actors' performances back into a filmic sense of real life.

Altman, Scorsese, and Cassavetes use many of the same techniques to achieve this effect. They often have the actors improvise dialogue, and sometimes film a rehearsal as the final take. Also, to gain this sense of the captured moment, Altman makes considerable use of overlapping dialogue and accidental noises that cover what is being said. In real conversation people interrupt each other, talk at the same time, can't be clearly heard, or, when alone, mumble to themselves. Altman's sound tracks are full of such natural conversation. He will go to even greater lengths to break down the barrier between film and life. He uses his cast both as people who are acting and as actors who are people. In *McCabe and Mrs. Miller* the prostitutes of Presbyterian Church have a birthday party. Altman instructed the actresses to invite those actors in the film whom they liked *as people* to attend the party. The resulting scene has a genuine quality that derives from both the actors' ability and the fact that they relate as people. In *Nashville*,

Altman has Elliot Gould and Julie Christie appear as themselves. The other characters react to them as movie stars, not as characters in the plot. It is difficult to tell if Gould and Christie are acting as themselves, are simply being themselves, or if the other actors are acting or responding as they would in real life. To achieve this effect Altman tends to use the same people in most of his films. The company has worked together so often that their human relationships contribute to their performances as actors. Elliot Gould, an extremely natural actor, or perhaps not an actor at all, best embodies Altman's idea. It is sometimes difficult to tell, in an Altman film, if there is a script, if anyone is acting, indeed if there is a director there at all.

Robert Altman began as a maker of industrial films and then spent fifteen years in television, directing three hundred hours of programming. He came to serious feature films late, making his first movie, *Images*, in 1970 when he was forty-five. Since then he has produced eight films, all clearly recognizable as Altman movies. Thematically, he explores and satirizes American folklore, whether the crazy commercial world of *Brewster McCloud*, the war in *MASH*, the romantic young outlaws in *Thieves Like Us*, the frontier in *McCabe and Mrs. Miller*, the private detective in *The Long Goodbye*, or the country-music scene in *Nashville*. Altman manages to explode the myth and show you what it was really like. Stylistically, his films are consistent. Altman's camera is voracious for detail; he makes us see everything, opens our eyes to things we might never notice. He assaults the senses with sound, color, shapes, textures, the natural motion and quality of the world he portrays. In *California Split* he captures the raw taste and feel of Las Vegas and the desperate rhythms of its citizens' empty lives. The opening scene of *McCabe and Mrs. Miller*—McCabe riding through the storm to gamble in the foul, noisy, smoke-filled den—is one of the most sensuously evocative scenes in films. Equally effective, *Nashville* bombards the viewer with the hysterical sights and sounds of a corrupt counterfeit culture, which is, by extension, the United States of America. His camera zooms in and out, skips, jumps, lingers, pans on everything. All details are equally arresting—faces, clothing, gestures, and surfaces of all kinds. It is film at its most visually expressive, where sound and image become, in combination, an immediate physical and emotional experience.

If it is possible to predict the future direction of American cinema, it may be, with Altman, away from tightly scripted, rigidly structured films toward freer, more immediate re-creations of the real moment—a coming together of life as it is lived and life as it is recorded. Watching future films, the viewer may find it increasingly difficult to tell which is more authentic—the motion picture or the street outside.

Index

DATE DUE

R L X JAN 1978				
SF N JAN 1984				
ONS AUG 1988				